Principal's Handbook
to Improve
Reading Instruction

Douglas P. Barnard, Ed.D.

*Assistant Superintendent
for Curriculum and Instruction
Mesa School District, Arizona*

Robert W. Hetzel, Ph.D.

*Assistant Superintendent
for Curriculum and Instruction
Catalina Foothills School District, Arizona*

with an introduction by

Carita A. Chapman

Ginn and Company

Design by Mona Zeftel
Cover design and photograph by Nikolai Goodman
Type collage by The Stonehand,
courtesy of The Bergen Record

Ginn and Company
Home Office: Lexington, Massachusetts 02173

0-663-41593-4

ACKNOWLEDGMENT

We acknowledge the very special thanks due our families for their patience, understanding, and encouragement during the writing of the manuscript. To Ann Gerhart, who typed the manuscript many times, we also express our thanks and appreciation.

TO

Mary
Russ
and
Christy

Becky
and
Andy

Contents

List of Charts

Preface

This book is not about reading. It is about how to improve reading services for children. It is meant to be a guide for the practicing administrator—especially the principal.

Schools generally use the same kinds of instructional materials, have comparable class sizes and equally experienced teachers, and normally deal with the same variables. Yet, achievement patterns can vary greatly even when these variables are controlled. The differences among schools have often been attributed to the influence of the principal, and we are convinced it is this person's performance—what he or she does and how he or she does it—that makes the difference.

Principals have been chastised for being office managers, for "merely" overseeing the running of a school, and rarely are recognized as instructional leaders. Moreover, critics seldom offer specific processes or advice to help the principal in becoming more effective in the role of leader. We have yet to know a principal who did not wish to be an instructional leader, but we have observed very few who had the necessary skills to achieve that status. It is not for lack of desire or concern on the principal's part that this situation exists, but rather because of lack of training and preparation for the role. Few if any colleges or universities offer training for administrators, especially principals, in the "processes" of effective management of a school's reading program.

Various solutions have been offered from outside the school, but they are often unrelated to the real problem. Systems analysis, time managment, goal analysis, and other management tools offer some aid, but often prove inadequate when we try to apply them, because of the lack of training of those charged with implementation and the complexities and pace of the contemporary school. Neglected in the quest for reading improvement has been a concern for the process of motivating and preparing people for the generation and implementation of solutions.

If the principal is the critical factor, then what is the difference between an effective and ineffective leader? This book reviews the management skills required by the principal, whether male or female, and the ways in which these skills can be applied to developing a school-wide reading program. Despite the generic pronoun used to refer to the principal throughout the handbook, we recognize that many of the most successful school administrators are women.

For those of you concerned about improving reading instruction in your schools or districts, this book defines a workable process for effecting change in order to improve reading services for children. The tactics have worked for others, and they can succeed for you!

D. P. B.
R. W. H.

Introduction

Reading is how we keep pace with the rapid explosion of knowledge. As this century draws to a close, we are seeing advances in communication, transportation, energy, technology, resource conservation, economic production, and many other areas. Understandably, society wants to know not only if the youth of today can use and extend these advances, but also if they will be prepared in the next millenium to control the abuses and misuses of technological change in a world with an ever increasing population.

This book takes a practical step forward in helping principals meet that challenge. The elementary school principal not only runs the school's plant and staff but also leads its most important program: reading. The principal is responsible for creating the climate in which youth can learn the essential reading skills necessary to cope with the needs of today and with the unpredictable and unforeseeable future. How to achieve that climate is the subject of this book.

Barnard and Hetzel, reading specialists and former principals, take as their thesis that what principals do and how they do it make a difference in how well children learn to read. Chapter One discusses how principals can give effective leadership to the instructional program through shared decision making with committee involvement. Everyone must help achieve a unified program to benefit the students. But to keep the reading program vital, it is the principal who must lead the way by focusing on goals, committing resources, and monitoring the reading program. The principal's responsibility is to facilitate teaching and learning.

After explaining how to achieve staff involvement in Chapter One, the authors show how to use this group to assess the effectiveness of the school's reading program. Chapter Two contains useful checklists to expedite the task. If any factor in the school reading program is found lacking, or there is a need for revitalization, the chapter has guidelines for developing the essential components of a school reading program: a philosophy; goals, objectives, materials; organization; monitoring; and feedback. It is the principal, the instructional leader, who gains the commitment and involvement of the school staff to a common reading program that will provide direction for children progressing through the elementary school. The right environment must be present to build the basic reading skills needed in the future.

Identification of an agreed upon school reading program philosophy and the reading skills to be taught leads naturally to the subject of assessment. Chapter Three suggests ways to judge the effectiveness of a program by comparing actual student achievement levels with expected levels. Not only is it important to know whether school performance, as determined by tests, is successful or not, but it is also crucial that the school examine test data for indications of problems and areas in need of improvement.

Chapter Four discusses in detail some of the important organizational factors that inhibit the reading program; things that test data do not indicate, such as staff instability, inadequate libraries and inappropriate use of the reading specialist. These and other areas, such as lack of early intervention and kindergarten programs, may require re-examination and revitalization of the existing programs.

The classroom is where the action is. Barnard and Hetzel stress the importance of both management of the classroom and management of the affective climate in Chapter Five. Not only is this chapter relevant for administrators, but classroom teachers could also learn from its contents. Knowing what makes a positive learning climate for systematic instruction appropriate to all learners provides a concrete concept of good classroom instruction. It is the role of the principal to insure quality reading services for children by monitoring the delivery of these services in the classroom—especially through the grouping of students and the use of the directed reading lesson. This climate will be conducive to more effective teaching and will promote greater learning of complex reading skills.

Where we find a deficiency in reading services for children, we must change and improve those services. Chapter Six provides the principal a process for effecting the needed change in a positive way, while dealing with the conflict and resistance that often accompany change.

The "human agenda" vital to change is also essential for the effective inservice programs discussed in Chapter Seven. While there is a general consensus that continued professional growth and improvement are necessary, this consensus is often negated because the people who should be involved often are not. The authors give detailed procedures for providing effective inservice, either immediately or on a continuous basis, for groups or for individual staff members, in order to improve services for children.

In Chapter Eight, Barnard and Hetzel show how to prevent reading material redundancy and neglect by suggesting procedures for the evaluation, selection, and management of textbook and supplemental materials. Too often, bookrooms are stocked with unused materials or there are "a million" books to teach one skill. Such situations can be eliminated by good selection procedures.

The ultimate goal of reading instruction is children who read and who want to read. Chapter Nine discusses activities other than direct reading instruction as a means of making reading visible and viable. In addition to teachers reading to their classes and extrinsic forms of recognition (charts, stars, awards, and so on) other in-school reading motivators, such as SSR and Junior Great Books, are discussed. Because much learning occurs outside the school, the authors suggest ways to involve parents and the community in helping to make reading important for students. These include ideas such as the Reading Fair, reading contracts, and Book Exchange Fair. Both in-school and out-of-school activities can be modified for use in either locale, but it is important to stress reading both in and out of school for the most effective reading achievement.

In their final chapter, Barnard and Hetzel provide a detailed view of the complex components of reading. The first part of the chapter defines reading, its major skills, and its major terms. The latter part of the chapter offers responses to typically asked questions about reading instruction. This "everything-you've-always-wanted-to-know-but-were-afraid-to-ask" chapter may well be read first by those unfamiliar with the subject of teaching reading. Obviously, these brief pages can offer only a cursory approach, but it should be more than enough to whet the appetite for more in-depth knowledge.

There has long been a need for a practical book to help the principal establish and maintain an effective reading program. This handbook contains important information for the new principal and at the same time provides practical suggestions and organizational schemes for the established principal who is implementing or improving a school reading program.

March, 1981

CARITA A. CHAPMAN, PH.D, Director
Bureau of Reading Services
Chicago Public Schools

Principal's Handbook
to Improve
Reading Instruction

1: The Principal: Leader or Administrator of the Reading Program?

Introduction

This book is based on the premise that what principals do makes a difference. Differences in achievement among schools are often inspired by a principal who can both administer the school and lead the instructional program. The impetus and guidance necessary to improve reading instruction for children depends greatly on leadership from the principal, and this is just the way it should be.

Today, the role of the principal is more complex and demanding than at any time in the past. Principals have to function under the pressures and constraints of federal and state mandates (such as P.L. 94–142), statewide competency testing, and due process in dealing with student behavior problems, while at the same time they must witness a waning of authority negotiated away to an increasing teacher militancy. In addition, the role of the principal has expanded to include the coordination of special education, public relations, staff development, and business management, much of which has little direct impact on instruction itself, which is the reason why schools exist. It is significant, however, that despite the reality of this atmosphere of increasing demands and complexities experienced by all principals, some schools consistently manifest better reading performance than other schools, and we believe that it is principals who make this difference in school performance.

With increasing frequency, these differences in achievement among schools are being attributed to the qualitative differences in leadership provided by principals. These differences are noted not only in the professional literature, by Weber (1), Venezky (2), Edmonds (3), Miller (4), and Barnard and Hetzel (5), but also in the public media. After completing a tour of schools in New York City, Carol Bellamy, the City Council President, came away convinced that the principal is the key. Bellamy states:

> One gets a sense of the spirit of the school by watching the principal. Most teachers
> are reasonably well prepared. A principal can get the best or the worst out of the
> teachers (6).

The research substantiates Bellamy's observations. Right to Read publications (7), (8), conclude that principals have an important impact on the overall performance and climate of the school. What they do and how they do it make a difference in how well children learn to read.

Power versus Influence

All principals are administrators by virtue of their positions, but not all possess the skills and attitudes required for leadership. The ability to unite a group to achieve a common goal is the very essence of leadership (9), and for the principal, this is demonstrated by his ability to unite a faculty and move them together to achieve a certain goal—in this case, improved reading instruction. Inherent in this process is the use of influence as opposed to power to convince rather than to force. Improved instruction cannot be administratively mandated. The pursuit of goals from a basis of power rather than of influence, and the emphasis on ''product'' to the neglect of process is contrary to effective leadership.

Power is the recognized right of an individual to make decisions despite objections (10). In school, power resides in the authority of the principal to control material resources through the budget and to control rewards and sanctions through supervision and evaluation. Such authority places the principal in a position either to motivate and guide a staff, or to discourage initiative, lower morale, and perpetuate mediocrity. Austin observes that in the more effective schools, principals rely on the power of expertise as opposed to the power of authority (by coercion or reward) and are seen by their staffs as ''instructional leaders,'' not ''administrative leaders'' (11).

The key prerequisite for leadership, then, is a willingness to share power and rely on influence and knowledge to arrive at decisions about the setting and pursuit of goals. Influence depends on trust, expertise, and involvement as opposed to the arbitrary exercise of authority. Unilateral administrative decisions with minimal input will only result in staff resistance and lower initiative (12).

Perhaps equally ineffective is the laissez-faire principal who holds power but abdicates this responsibility entirely by turning decision making over to the staff with no attempt to provide guidance or influence (13). The effective principal is neither an autocrat nor a laissez-faire administrator.

Sharing Decisions: The Key

No single leadership function is more vital to improving instruction than decision making. Failure to develop a thoughtful process for decision making indicates the absence of leadership. Principals must recognize that their responsibility is to see that decisions are made effectively, which is not the same thing as making decisions themselves. In his classic work on administration, Griffiths goes so far as to include the following as a major proposition of his theory:

> The effectiveness of the chief executive is inversely proportional to the number of decisions which he must personally make concerning the organization. It is not the function of the chief executive to make decisions; it is his function to monitor the decision-making process to make certain that it performs at the optimum level (14).

He goes on to say that decisions will be more effective if administrators see themselves as controllers of the process rather than as makers of decisions (15).

Effective decision making takes into account acceptance, probable resistance, implementation, and follow-through. These variables are best dealt with by involving the teachers and other staff who must make the decisions work. Likert emphasizes the value of involvement:

> Through group decision-making each member feels fully identified with each decision and highly motivated to execute it fully. The over-all performance of the group, as a consequence, is even better than the excellent quality of the decision (16).

English heartily concurs:

> There is no longer any question whether he will decide to involve other groups. The question is how and under what conditions can maximum involvement improve the quality of the instructional program (17).

The thesis of this book is straightforward and simple. Leaders understand how and when to involve people and they place a high value on this process. Principals who lack the confidence or skill to trust and interact with their staff will not make successful leaders. The remainder of this book is devoted to discussing the techniques and information required to involve a staff in improving reading services for children, and examples are provided. Involving staff in decision-making activity requires, first of all, proficiency in the organization and use of committees and in the conduct of meetings.

The Reading Program: Necessary Leadership Skills

COMMITTEE CRAFT

There are three basic settings for making decisions:

1. groups that are set up to function without the principal as leader;

2. groups where the principal participates as a member; or

3. singly, where the decision is made directly by the principal.

The latter setting should be discouraged when resulting decisions affect the majority of the staff. The decision-making groups described in settings 1 and 2 are more commonly—sometimes infamously—known as committees. Given the often deserved disrepute into which committees can fall, a thorough understanding of the operation of committees is vitally important to effective leadership.

COMMITTEE OR NO COMMITTEE A committee functioning without the principal as an active participant will succeed to the degree that the committee members consider the task assigned them significant. So the principal's first consideration should be whether a committee is the best format to use to accomplish a given task. In making this judgment, the primary question is whether the principal already has a final outcome or decision in mind. If so, he should *not* form a committee. People resent spending valuable time and energy producing the inevitable, and they should *not* be convened merely to debate a foregone conclusion. A rule of thumb for administrators to use in their determinations is to ask themselves if they are willing to accept the final report or decision of the committee as defined in the charge. If not, then a committee is not the best means for accomplishing the task at hand.

A second consideration is whether enough time and/or expertise are available to allow a committee to function successfully. It is a faulty assumption that group decisions are necessarily better than individual decisions, especially if time is a critical factor (19). When expertise is lacking, deliberation rarely results in worthwhile decisions. Committee members could possibly inform themselves while serving on the committee, but again, if time and/or expertise are a constraint, a different approach might well be warranted. Involvement for involvement's sake is only counter-productive.

FORMING THE COMMITTEE Once you decide to form a committee, you need to state its purpose clearly in order that its size and membership can be realistically set. The composition and size of a committee are usually determined by one or all of the following requirements:

1. Having a representative group
2. Developing a sense of ownership
3. Contributing expertise and knowledge

We need to examine the assumptions underlying these requirements. It is a faulty assumption that people assigned to represent others will actually do so. Representation requires the committee member to solicit views and report back to those represented. Unfortunately, in many cases the committee member represents no more than his own personal views and makes little effort to gather input from others. Therefore, the chair needs to monitor, formally or informally, whether committee members are communicating regularly with their constituency. Committee members can accomplish this by 1) keeping a log of efforts in soliciting and furnishing data to others, and 2) giving oral or written reports to the committee.

Another false premise is that just by virtue of being on a committee, members will assume "ownership" of its final "product" or decision. Their commitment and follow-through are directly proportional to the degree that the committee outcome affects their responsibilities and vested interests. Therefore, committee members should be people who have something to gain by completing the task.

In addition to this vested interest, the people assigned should have the knowledge, energy, and time required to carry out the task. One problem, however, is that the most energetic and knowledgeable members of the organization tend to serve on too many committees. It is important that committee assignments neither overburden nor overlook specific members of the organization, whether it is a single school or an entire system. And if prospective committee members lack sufficient expertise or knowledge, an effort should be made, through inservice training, to give them the minimum background information they need to function effectively.

DIRECTING THE CHAIR Once the committee has been formed, the principal should charge the chair with a specific task. Committees often waste time setting up goals and identifying their purpose when all this should be thought out before the first meeting.

The administrator should appoint the chair and give that person the responsibility for managing the committee. Specific information the chair needs includes the following:

1. Purpose and goal
2. Timeline for completing the task
3. Resources available (people, money, time, etc.)
4. Form of the committee's final product and/or evidence of its completed task.

CLOSURE Often, a major morale problem in committee work is the absence of closure, the formal termination of the committee. It is critical that the administrator report to the committee members his or her final decision or reactions to the committee's efforts. In the same way, it is imperative that committee members report back to any groups represented.

The checklist below can serve as a useful guide for principals in assessing their needs and skills in committee craft.

Committee Craft Checklist

Committee or No Committee?

1. Do I have a final decision or "product" in mind?   Yes   No
2. Am I willing to accept the final product or decision of the committee?   Yes   No
3. Is adequate expertise available for the task?   Yes   No
4. Is time a constraint?   Yes   No

Purpose of the Committee

1. To reach a decision   Yes   No
2. To make a recommendation   Yes   No
3. To produce a product   Yes   No
4. To gather data for others   Yes   No
5. To serve as a governing body   Yes   No

Representation on the Committee

1. Do I want representative groups?   Yes   No
2. Is there a need to develop a sense of ownership?   Yes   No
3. Will adequate expertise and knowledge available be brought to bear?   Yes   No

Instructions to the Chairperson

1. Have I furnished the purpose of the committee in writing, and is it feasible?   Yes   No
2. Did I provide a timeline for task completion?   Yes   No
3. Did I list the resources available?   Yes   No
4. Did I provide criteria for the final product?   Yes   No
5. Did I set a deadline?   Yes   No

THE LEADER AS COMMITTEE MEMBER The principal's participation in a group or committee within the school is significant and lends greater status and importance to the group's task. However, the principal must guard against dominating the group and stifling participation. This requires a sensitivity to his role within the group.

The effective leader does not impose personal views, but demonstrates a patience and willingness to sacrifice time for the benefits of participative decision making. This means that he asks questions and makes speculative rather than direct statements. He provides the group with information and technical expertise, including outside resource people. The leader delegates responsibility within the group and volunteers for some of the more mundane assignments. And finally, by following others at the appropriate time, the principal helps others develop leadership skills and provides a model of good participant behavior. Here is a list to help you in periodically checking your group leadership abilities.

Group Leadership: Points to Ponder

Do I dominate or share in discussions?

Do I guide with prompting questions and speculative comments or with direct statements and declaratives?

Do I cite research and call on expertise or rest solely on my experience or opinion?

Do I share the mundane and routine tasks as well as the more interesting and important ones?

Do I follow the way I would like others to follow?

HOW WELL IS THE COMMITTEE PERFORMING? A working group needs feedback for at least two reasons: to know whether it is progressing toward its goal and to learn how it is functioning collectively. The leader provides goal feedback by keeping a continuous written record of events and their relationship to the anticipated final product. Minutes and summaries at the conclusion of meetings help to keep the goal in focus and the end in sight. To sustain effort you must be able to feel progress is being made.

Feedback to the committee on how effectively it is functioning as a group can be obtained through this simple anonymous climate survey:

Group Climate Survey

In the group . . .	ALL THE TIME	SOMETIMES	NEVER
1. my opinions are respected.			
2. communication is open.			
3. my contributions are accepted.			
4. my time is wasted.			
5. the task is well understood.			
6. people respect one another.			

Effective Meetings

That often-maligned institution, the meeting, is the essential ingredient in any decision-making process. Meetings by themselves are neither good or bad, but their leadership can be. The primary rule for a successful meeting is to know its purpose; if none is clearly defined, a meeting should not be held. The second major rule is to inform the group involved of the purpose of the meeting, and at its close, to restate that purpose and decide whether it has been achieved.

Following a few simple guidelines can help make meetings more successful in accomplishing the job at hand in a minimum amount of time. Try to remember that it isn't *meetings* that people resent, but rather *wasting time*. These suggestions can help:

1. If at all possible, schedule meetings with self-imposed deadlines—such as before lunch or before school—so they do not go on endlessly.

2. Small groups tend to work better than large ones, so have only essential people at the meeting.

3. Inform people beforehand of the meeting's purpose and agenda so that they know what they will be doing.

4. Start on time; latecomers will catch on.

5. Restate the purpose, work from the agenda, and stick to it.

6. Summarize what has been accomplished before adjourning.

7. Thank people for meeting. *Recognize* their efforts.

8. Provide a written summary of decisions and questions as soon as possible after the meeting.

Instructional leadership depends on involving people in focusing on a goal and moving towards it. Committees and meetings form a part of this general process and demand organizational know-how from the principal in order to be effective. There are, however, other elements fundamental to improving a reading program.

Leading the Reading Program

Despite common opinion, the expertise required of a principal to improve the reading program does not necessarily lie in the field of theory and methodology. More often, what is required is the ability to focus on a goal, commit resources, and monitor the program (20).

FOCUSING ON THE GOAL

An organizational goal must be advertised if the organization's members are to recognize and accept it. If improvement of reading is the goal, then that topic must be kept in the forefront of all activities in the school. Unless the goal is uppermost in the minds of those who must achieve it, it tends to be displaced by daily concerns and crises, and will seldom be attained.

A principal can do much to keep the goal clearly in focus. It is through his actions, not only words, that true commitment shows itself. The administrator's attendance at meetings about reading within both the school and the district is important. This demonstrates to teachers that he is interested and concerned, and thus spurs them on to redouble their own efforts. Articles placed in the mailboxes and on the bulletin board, as well as a few minutes taken at a staff meeting to highlight a teacher's ideas or efforts in reading, are also good ways to keep the goal in the forefront. Perhaps no single act on the principal's part will go further toward goal achievement than a well-deserved compliment or word of praise for someone's efforts.

RESOURCE COMMITMENT

Resource commitment is unquestionably the most dramatic reflection of the priority of a goal within a school or district; it reinforces both the stated and tacit goals of an institution. The amount of resources (time, space, personnel, and materials) allocated, and the preference reading receives in the budget tell the staff more about the significance of the reading program than anything the principal can say.

Enthusiasm is contagious, and a principal who constantly searches for, borrows, and secures needed resources such as books or volunteers to support daily activities will excite teachers. Teachers sense this effort and work harder to achieve goals. Most importantly, how a principal allots his own valuable time will say a great deal about the importance he attaches to the reading program. If the principal cannot find time for reading, it must be unimportant. But if the principal is actively involved, attending meetings, visiting classrooms, securing resources, and working with staff members, then the staff sees that the reading program goal is significant and important.

PROGRAM MONITORING: ESTABLISHING PERSONAL COMMITMENT AND DIRECTION

Monitoring the reading program is a step often overlooked, yet it holds the greatest promise for program improvement. The monitoring plan reinforces goals by recognizing them; it emphasizes the substance and significance of teachers' work. It offers an opportunity to reward performance, and it helps teachers by resolving any problems that have arisen.

A leader must know how to involve others in reaching goals. Expectations vital to achieving goals need to be made personal. They have to be translated from the institutional level to the individual level. This promotes personal commitment and "ownership" of the tasks required to achieve the goal. People want to know specifically what is expected of them during the course of their daily routine. There are several ways a principal can raise the personal expectations of the staff about the reading program.

The first step is to identify those tasks or components teachers feel are essential in providing effective reading instruction for children. If the goal is improvement, there are certain steps to which each individual should be committed. Here is a list that can serve as a starting point for staff discussion:

1. Specific, written performance objectives for the reading curriculum

2. A test for program placement and a diagnostic assessment related to performance objectives to identify subskill needs of all students

3. Directed reading lessons to meet specific objectives for the core or basic reading program

4. Materials organized for each skill objective (materials correlated to objectives)

5. A classroom management plan (record keeping) that allows the teacher to group according to need and to provide for different levels of instruction and learning rates

6. An evaluation system for knowing when each student has mastered the necessary skills (criterion-referenced tests)

7. An explanation of the reading program to the principal and/or parents that shows how tasks 1–6 are completed

Ask teachers whether these tasks will enchance achievement. Add or delete tasks. Ask the staff to scrutinize, refine, and agree on the tasks remaining. Such involvement and agreement result in the emergence of personal expectations and commitment to them.

Once the list is complete, establish a timeline and a schedule for monitoring. The principal can then meet with individuals or teams to determine whether the tasks are being completed on time. If critical tasks have not begun, the principal should assist teachers in whatever way possible. Such help should not be given grudgingly, as a remedy for failure, but rather as a cooperative gesture for joint success. This process means significant discussion about the essence of improving reading. It means going to the heart of the matter—what the teacher actually does in the classroom.

One of the purposes of the monitoring process is to determine the rate and tempo of change in the school, which should not exceed the ability, energy, and general readiness of the staff. Effective monitoring comes through constant interaction with, and encouragement of, teachers, so that they feel progressively freer to express their concerns, anxieties, and hopes for program improvement. Being aware of, and attending to, teachers' needs are important components in promoting professional rapport and growth. In summary, if reading instruction is to improve, the principal must assume the role of instructional leader and resist limiting himself to merely managing the school. The principal must take this first step to improvement. The children depend on it.

REFERENCES

1. George Webber, *Inner-City Children Can Be Taught to Read: Four Successful Schools,* Council for Basic Education, Occasional Paper No. 18, Washington, D.C., October, 1971.

2. Richard Venezky, "Reflections—The Child Learning to Read," *Language Arts,* Vol. 56, No. 8, (November/December, 1979), pp. 888–889.

3. Ronald Edmonds, "Effective Schools for the Urban Poor," *Educational Leadership,* Vol. 87, No. 1, (October, 1979), p. 17.

4. William C. Miller, "Can a Principal's Improved Behavior Result in Higher Pupil Achievement?" *Educational Leadership,* (February, 1976), pp. 336–338.

5. Douglas Barnard and Robert Hetzel, "The Principal's Role in Reading Instruction," *The Reading Teacher,* Vol. 29, No. 4, (January, 1976) pp. 386–388.

6. Carol Bellamy, *The New York Times,* May 29, 1979.

7. Right to Read, *Principals and Reading Specialists: Their Impact on Reading Instruction.* Newark: International Reading Association, Vol. 3, No. 2, (December, 1976).

8. Right to Read, *Reporting on Reading, Administrators Emphasize Reading.* (St. Louis: CEMREL, (September, 1978).

9

9. David G. Bowers and Stanley E. Seashore, "Predicting Organizational Effectiveness with a Four Factor Theory of Leadership," in *Readings in Organizational Behavior and Human Performance*, Eds. L. L. Cummings and W. E. Scott. Homewood, Illinois: The Dorsey Press, 1969, pp. 599-600.

10. Daniel E. Griffiths, "Administration as Decision-Making," in *Organization and Human Behavior: Focus on Schools*, Eds. Fred D. Carver and Thomas J. Sergiovanni. New York: McGraw-Hill, 1969, pp. 145-146.

11. Gilbert R. Austin, "Exemplary Schools and the Search for Effectiveness," *Educational Leadership*, Vol. 37, No. 1, (October, 1979), p. 12.

12. Jacob W. Getzels, James M. Lipham, and Robald F. Campbell, *Educational Administration as a Social Process: Theory, Research, Practice*. New York: Harper and Row, pp. 36-39.

13. Ibid., pp. 38-39.

14. Daniel Griffiths, *Administrative Theory*. New York: Appleton-Century-Crofts, 1959, pp. 71-91.

15. Ibid, pp. 71-91.

16. Rensis Likert, "The Nature of Highly Effective Groups," in *Organization and Human Behavior: Focus on Schools*, Eds., Fred D. Carver and Thomas J. Sergiovanni. New York: McGraw-Hill, 1969, pp. 360-361.

17. Fenwick W. English, *School Organization and Management*. Worthington, Ohio: Charles A. Jones, 1975, p. 26.

18. Douglas P. Barnard and Robert W. Hetzel, "A Process for Committeeship," *The Clearing House*, Vol. 5, No. 1, (September, 1978), pp. 32-34.

19. Normal R. F. Maier, "Assets and Liabilities in Group Problem Solving: The Need for an Integrated Function," in *Reading in Organizational Behavior and Human Performance*, Eds., L. L. Cummings and W. E. Scott. Homewood, Illinois: The Dorsey Press, 1969, p. 584.

20. Douglas Barnard and Robert Hetzel, op. cit., pp. 386-388.

2: Does My School Have a Reading Program?

Introduction

The *reading program* is frequently discussed as if everyone understood the term the same way. A *program* is a unification of what teachers do, according to what sequence, with what tools, under what conditions or structure, and with some agreement as to the expectations that will result from these efforts. Too frequently, educational literature emphasizes the classroom reading program to the neglect of a unified perception of the whole school program. In order to offer the best reading services to all children, we must consolidate the entire program. *The major concept of a school reading program is that it implies unity of purpose between and among staff members, as opposed to the independence of classroom programs operating in isolation from one another.*

When we unify classroom programs into a *school* program, reading services are more fully used. Children no longer simply pass from teacher to teacher, each with his or her own reading program, but progress through a unified reading system. According to Avery (1), such a program prevents readers from becoming the victims of a fragmented approach, receiving bits and pieces by divergent routes of reading instruction. As Singer emphasizes, ''It is the total staff using a systematic instructional program in which they are trained and competent that seems to make the difference in a school's reading achievement'' (2).

Assessing the School Reading Program

Neither legislators, parents, nor others outside the school system will improve the school reading program, but rather those teachers directly involved with children. If teachers are expected to make the changes resulting from program evaluation, they must be involved in the assessment. And being directly involved in the self-assessment process, teachers discover program needs for themselves. This is far preferable to their being told of shortcomings or omissions—comments not always accepted as constructive criticism.

By using the following assessment process and guide, the principal can involve staff members in creating an awareness of the strengths, weaknesses, and needs of the school reading program. The key is the process as it results in personal commitment for program improvement.

11

This process begins with individual staff members and the principal completing the following self-assessment guide independently. The guides are then collected and tabulated by item and grade level. Upon completion of this task, the reading director or consultant is also invited to complete the guide.

The principal then compares the results from the consultants and teachers with his own assessment, and identifies any discrepancies that may indicate problems. By emphasizing inconsistencies and creating an awareness of problems, these data help transfer the responsibility for problem solving from the principal to the teachers—from an *institutional* level to a *personal* level. It is essential that assessment results be shared with teachers as soon as possible after all information has been collected. Together, teachers and principals can then set goals and establish plans for solving any problems.

Figure 2–1: Present School Status in Reading

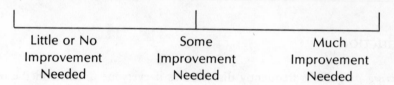

| Little or No Improvement Needed | Some Improvement Needed | Much Improvement Needed |

School Reading Program Assessment Guide

School's General Program

1. Is there a common school philosophy for reading instruction? Yes No

2. Is there a scope and sequence of reading goals and objectives? Yes No

3. Is the core or basic reading program consistent at the primary level? Yes No

4. Is the core or basic reading program consistent at the intermediate level? Yes No

5. Is daily reading instruction provided for an appropriate length of time at each grade level (primary—2 hours daily, upper grades—1 hour daily)? Yes No

6. Is there program coordination between or among the primary grades? Yes No

7. Is there program coordination between or among the intermediate grades? Yes No

8. Is there program coordination between the primary and upper grades? Yes No

9. Is an individual reading record passed yearly from teacher to teacher, showing progress in the core or basic reading program? Yes No

10. Are students allowed to progress to the next grade-level material (continuous progress)? Yes No

11. Does the program emphasize prevention of reading problems by allocation of resources at the primary level, versus remedial work at higher grade levels? Yes No

12. Is there continuous effort to upgrade teacher skills through district inservice? Yes No

General Classroom Procedures

13. Are students placed in the core or basic instructional materials level based on Initial Reading Inventory (IRI) Placement tests and previous records by the third week of school (See Appendix B)? Yes No

14. Are students grouped for instruction according to individual skill needs? Yes No

15. Does the teacher conduct directed lessons for the basic reading program for each new story introduced? Yes No

16. Do students receive at least twice a week, special skills-directed instruction related to specific objectives of the reading program? Yes No

13

17. Does the teacher provide short and meaningful drill work (for example, sight words) as needed?　　　　　　Yes　　No

18. Do students read silently on a daily basis?　　　　　Yes　　No

19. Do students read daily?　　　　　　　　　　　　Yes　　No

20. Do low-achieving students receive additional directed instruction daily?　　　　　　　　　　　　　　　Yes　　No

21. Are students' needs and progress monitored and is a recording system used?　　　　　　　　　　　Yes　　No

22. Do students receive adequate instruction before independent activities?　　　　　　　　　　　　　Yes　　No

23. Do students progress at a rate at which they can master the material? The following guide may be used:　　Yes　　No

　　a. Top Group—2 stories per week,
　　　no more than 2 errors per page.

　　b. Middle Group—1 story per week,
　　　no more than 2 errors per page.

　　c. Bottom Group—sight word mastery
　　　determines progress; 1st-graders
　　　in this group shoud be in pre-
　　　primers by January.

24. Are enrichment activities in reading provided on a weekly basis?　　　　　　　　　　　　　　　　Yes　　No

Achievement Results (Standards are *suggested*, and should be adjusted for individual schools.)

25. Do entering first-grade students have a 90% average score in the top two quartiles of an established reading readiness test?　　　　　　　　　　　　　　Yes　　No

26. Do stable third-grade students (those in school since the first grade) score at 3.0 or higher?　　　　　Yes　　No

27. On criterion-referenced tests, do students have mastery of 80% of each reading objective?　　　　　　Yes　　No

Any questions answered *no* could indicate possible problems and these areas should be examined.

If the data indicate a need for much improvement, the staff should begin the following process for revamping and unifying the school program. This process involves a series of meetings in which one session is devoted to each component listed below.

Components of a School Reading Program

The authors have identified five components essential to a school reading program:

1. an instructional philosophy,

2. the identification of goals, objectives and material,

3. the ordering of instructional tasks,

4. the monitoring of the program, and

5. the establishment of a renewal system (3).

These are the elements that unify the school reading program into a productive, supportive service for all students.

Developing a School Reading Program

EVOLVING A PHILOSOPHY

A reading instruction philosophy is a *belief* about *how* reading should be taught. A philosophy is important because it guides, if not dictates, decisions about goals and objectives, materials, and the organizing and ordering of instructional tasks. Every teacher has a philosophy, whether expressed or not, that guides her or his daily activities and practices in the classroom.

If teachers have different philosophies, students will be faced with different approaches that can result in learning gaps as they progress through the grades. With contradictory teaching, progress slows—seriously so for the bottom third of a class. A single basal reading system helps prevent such a disadvantage for students, but it is only a partial remedy, because there is no substitute for good teaching, even when quality materials are available. It is critical, however, that all teachers support a common philosophy.

There are two basic methods a principal can employ with the staff to evolve a school reading program philosophy. In one approach, the principal prepares a list of statements that reflect various philosophical approaches; the staff then reacts to each statement and eventually arrives at a consensus. Another approach requires the staff to generate statements that when compiled result in a philosophy.

CONSENSUS TECHNIQUE   The principal divides the staff into groups of three to five teachers, asking them to select one member as clerk and spokesperson for each group. He places on the chalkboard or overhead projector, or distributes, a list of statements on how reading should be taught. We have provided a sample list.

How to Teach Reading

1. ____ We believe in, and are committed to, having every student read at a level commensurate with his or her ability.

2. ____ We believe in, and are committed to, continuous progress for each individual.

3. ____ We believe that every child should be an independent reader.

4. ____ We believe that every child should be successful 90% of the time in daily assignments.

5. ____ We believe that initial reading instruction should be analytical (words to letters).

6. ____ We believe that initial reading instruction should be synthetic (letters to words).

7. ____ We believe in an eclectic approach.

8. ____ We believe that students should be homogeneously grouped.

9. ____ We believe that students should be heterogeneously grouped.

10. ____ We believe in small-group instruction.

11. ____ We believe in large-group instruction.

12. ____ We believe in flexible grouping by skill needs.

13. ____ We believe that students should be using core materials based on an IRI or placement test on those materials.

14. ____ We believe that students' subskill needs should be identified.

15. ____ We believe in the mastery learning concept and we believe that 95% of the students can achieve mastery by altering time.

16. ____ We believe that a child's progress should be monitored.

ALTERNATIVE APPROACH   The alternative method is to ask the groups to generate, in a brainstorming session, their own list of beliefs about reading instruction. The statements generated can then be dealt with using the process described above.

After allowing time for discussion of each statement, led by the clerk of each group, the principal solicits the responses from each clerk. The clerk reports a consensus or no consensus for each item. The principal should allow only a few minutes for each question and go on to the next one to avoid lengthy, unproductive discussions. The goal is to reach a consensus of opinion. After all groups have stated their beliefs, the principal should discuss with the total group any points of disagreement and seek a synthesis in which the total staff can support a common concept. The principal then prepares a one- or two-paragraph statement of philosophy representing what the teachers believe about reading, and distributes it to all participants, asking for any revision before adoption. It is crucial that the *total* staff feel involved in, and thereby committed to, the resulting philosophical statement.

GOALS, OBJECTIVES, AND MATERIALS

The reading curriculum is a list of the reading goals and objectives that educators believe children should master to become independent readers. These skills (see Appendix A) are fairly standard in most school districts and basal reading systems, although the sequence may vary. A reading curriculum containing goals and objectives in a scope and sequence format is essential. Difficulties that may arise, disrupting student progress, are probably not the fault of the curriculum itself, but of its interpretation. There must be agreement on goals, objectives, and materials used, and once again the principal should solicit staff comment.

Using the goals and objectives list in Appendix A, the basic core program, or a school-adopted list, the principal again divides the group into subgroups and asks the following kinds of questions:

1. Does our philosophy match our goals and objectives?

2. What materials do we use in our school?

3. Do the materials we are now using complement our objectives?

4. Do we have materials for the top and bottom thirds of our classes?

5. Should we use one core set of materials through the primary grades and supplement these as needed, or should we use a variety of procedures?

After five or ten minutes of group discussion on each question, the principal calls on the group spokesperson to report the decisions of each group. After all groups have responded, the principal discusses any disagreements in an effort to arrive at a conclusion that the majority of the teachers can support. He should then prepare a statement listing the basic materials that constitute, and are used in, the school reading program. This narrative should then be added to the philosophical statement and distributed to the teachers for their analysis and criticism before the next meeting.

ORDERING INSTRUCTIONAL TASKS

An organizational system provides guidelines and lists the teacher tasks necessary to implement the reading curriculum year by year. When the instructional sequence for the students is determined, all participants are aware of *what* should occur *when,* and *who* is responsible for each step in the program. This system coordinates the reading services and clarifies vertical and horizontal relationships among staff and administration.

In the series of meetings required to formulate a school reading program, the most critical is the meeting to establish the teacher's tasks, and their order, for each level of the program. The objective here is to examine what happens to a child as he or she enters school and progresses through each grade. The principal again divides the teachers into groups, and asks the following questions:

1. What is the first instructional task a teacher performs at the beginning of the year?

2. What is the second task?

3. What steps must I take in teaching a reading lesson?

This procedure should continue until all tasks are identified, and should be used for all grade groups in attendance. Write the following headings on the chalkboard and fill in the tasks as they are identified by the groups. The rest of the form can be completed by the entire staff once the tasks are identified and agreed on. The principal may then ask such questions as, ''Who should perform the task? By when? Who should know the task has been accomplished?''

Figure 2–2: Sample Instructional Tasks Organization

Task	Responsibility	Date Completed	Notify
Administer IRI to All Students	Teacher & Reading Teacher	End of First Two Weeks of School	Primary Chair and Principal
Administer District Subskill Tests	Reading Teacher	End of First Two Weeks of School	Primary Chair and Principal

This kind of organization clarifies who does what (and when), and who is to be notified upon completion of the task. It is a timeline—a sequence of events necessary to provide maximum reading services. The chart should be prepared and added to the other program components for distribution before the next meeting.

PROGRAM MONITORING

The only way to learn if the program components—the philosophy, goals, objectives, and organizational plan—are actually being implemented and working is to check. Any program must be monitored to insure that the system is operational and that goals are being achieved with minimal frustration for students and teachers. Ongoing evaluation and actual observance of the operation of the program are necessary. The principal's main responsibility is to check teacher performance against the objectives, and to intervene when problems are identified. The principal's failure to do so can mark the first stage of the degeneration of the reading program.

RENEWAL SYSTEM

A renewal system is necessary both to maintain and to continually improve services for students. This entails reviewing the expectations of teachers in reading instruction, being constantly alert for problems, and arranging training sessions to help teachers become more effective. As programs are implemented and monitored, the training needs of teachers become apparent. This is the ideal time for intervention by consultants or other specialists, or the use of added resources. A renewal system gives teachers the opportunity to identify their own needs and to gain knowledge and expertise. This is an inherent and valuable part of the total school reading program.

The following questions should help the principal establish a monitoring and renewal system. Once teacher tasks and expectations are agreed on, these tasks are monitored to assure that they are performed according to agreement. Some questions that can be posed to teachers include:

1. How do we monitor the learning of students?

2. What steps do we take if a child does not appear to be learning?

3. If all else fails, whom can we turn to for assistance?

4. If we want demonstrations or workshops, what resources are available?

Allow time to discuss these questions and reach a consensus. Then add the procedures agreed on to the statements on the other components and distribute the combined statements to staff members.

SCHOOL PROGRAM DESCRIPTION

The result of this process should be a written description of each component of the school reading program. Because such reports are the result of staff consensus, they are valuable from the standpoint of personal involvement in, and commitment to, any changes needed. Staff awareness increases, teachers "own" the program, and goals become individual and personal. Your school now has a reading program that provides direction and defines program expectations. More important it helps provide systematic instruction for children as they progress through the grades.

REFERENCES

1. Paul J. Avery, "The Obligations of School Administrators to the Reading Program," in *Administrators and Reading,* Ed. Thorsten R. Carlson. New York: Harcourt, Brace and Jovanovich, 1972, p. 14.

2. Harry Singer, "Resolving Curricular Conflicts in the 1970's: Modifying the Hypothesis, It's the Teacher Who Makes the Difference in Reading Achievement," *Language Arts,* Vol. 54, No. 2, (February, 1977), p. 162.

3. Douglas Barnard, "A Process to Revitalize the School Reading Program," *The Florida Reading Quarterly,* Vol. 8, (May, 1974).

3: Is the Reading Program Working?

Introduction

Unfortunately, too often the community and central administration judge a school on the basis of its reading achievement scores alone. The practice, common in many states, of publishing reading scores in local newspapers has led various publics to draw conclusions, valid or not, about the overall academic effectiveness of the school. The danger in publishing reading scores is that they are subject to misinterpretation. Often the variables influencing the scores are not considered, nor do the scores by themselves accurately reflect the effort or expertise of a school staff and principal. Nevertheless, this publicizing trend will probably continue as more states legislate minimum competency programs and the pressure for improved scores persists.

The first step in such a case is to determine if, indeed, a reading problem exists. If it does, a principal's task is then to create awareness among teachers of the problem, and explain that responsibility for its resolution rests with the total staff, including the principal. It is a *collective* problem. If reading scores are to improve, the obligation for improving them has to be assumed at the school level by all involved, with the central office providing resources, training, and monitoring activities in support.

At the school level, the principal has the authority and duty to evaluate the reading program. The available data vary from district to district and range from highly sophisticated testing programs to no scores at all. Similarly, program analysis procedures range from simple pre-post comparisons to complex analyses of the multiple variables in contemporary elementary schools. Even with limited information at hand, however, there are procedures a principal can use to determine if the school has a reading problem. For every school, there are sources of data and ways of evaluating the reading program.

Discrepancy Analysis

In trying to determine if there is a reading problem, the principal should ask two questions. At what level are the students actually reading, and at what level should they be reading?[2] A gap—a discrepancy—between the two levels indicates a problem. How sophisticated the analysis for discovering differences is depends on the data and expertise available. The crucial point, however, is to discover if a discrepancy exists—and to what degree—so that a plan of action can be made. There are several sources a principal can consult in order to discover a possible discrepancy.

Data for Determining Actual versus Expected Performance

INFORMAL READING INVENTORY

The minimum data available from school reading program records would include the informal reading inventory* and/or the basal reading placement test results, which show the level at which students are reading within the program. Even though this information is limited, it can be used to flag a potential problem.

Usually, it is expected that about two-thirds of a class will complete one grade-level textbook within one school year. Above-average students will probably do more, and below-average students less, but about two-thirds or more should make a year's progress within the reading program. Data on where students are placed in the reading program at the beginning of a school year can then be compared to data on where those same students are at the end of the year or at the beginning of the following year. An assessment of progress can then be made.

STANDARDIZED TESTS AND NORMS

The data provided by administering a standardized reading test are very helpful in assessing the effectiveness of the reading program. The distribution of test scores compared to the normal distribution curve gives at least one indication of how well the program is working. The distribution of reading scores of students should roughly parallel the distribution in Figure 3–1.

Figure 3–1:   Student Reading Scores Distribution

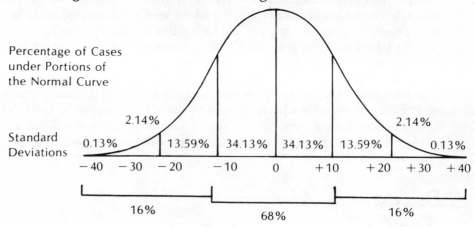

Percentage of Cases under Portions of the Normal Curve

Standard Deviations

2.14%   2.14%

0.13%   13.59%   34.13%   34.13%   13.59%   0.13%

−40   −30   −20   −10   0   +10   +20   +30   +40

16%   68%   16%

* See Chapter Ten, item 32, page 102, for a detailed discussion of the IRI.

That is, about 16 percent of the students should be at both the lower and higher ends, and about 68 percent should fall within one standard deviation of the center. Consider the following examples:

Table 3–1: Sample Reading Scores Distribution

Number of Students in:	Low 16%	Average 68%	High 16%
School or Classroom A	13	66	21
School or Classroom B	25	50	25
School or Classroom C	11	67	22

Example A is representative of a school or classroom performing well, especially with the above-average students. In example B, instruction appears to be geared toward the brighter students, with less emphasis on below-average students. School or classroom C is performing well across the board.

If test scores are reported in stanines, the same general distribution curve could be used, with the three major percents at 23, 54, and 23, instead of 16, 68, and 16. That is, stanines 1, 2, and 3 are low; 4, 5, and 6 are average; and 7, 8, and 9 are considered high, as illustrated in the table below.

By grouping the number of students scoring in each stanine and computing a percentage, you can analyze the data. Notice, however, that the groups compared in the examples below are students whose scores approximate the normal population on a given test. Interpolations would be needed if the population does not fit a norm population and scores are skewed to the right or left of the mean.

INTELLIGENCE AND STANDARDIZED READING TEST SCORES

If the school uses intelligence tests, then the average of the intelligence scores for a particular class can serve as a model of expectations for reading achievement. That is, if the

Table 3–2: Reading Scores Distribution by Stanines

Stanine	% of Normal Population	Percentage of Children by Grade Level, Class, or School Within Each Category		
7, 8, 9 High	23%	31%	33%	34%
4, 5, 6 Average	54%	49%	34%	50%
1, 2, 3 Low	23%	20%	33%	16%
		A	B	C
		School/Classroom		

average second-grade intelligence score is 100, which is the norm, then normal placement and progress in the reading program should be about what publishers state as
typical for that program. On a standardized test, this group should score close to grade-
level and national norms for the test. Intelligence tests administered in the latter part of
the second, or the beginning of the third grade probably give a better indication of the
total school population than do intelligence scores obtained at the upper elementary
grades. At upper-grade levels, intelligence tests become reading tests, as performance
begins to depend on the ability to read.

Consider each of the following possible situations for third-grade classes that were
tested in the late spring. The national norm, in this case, would be 3.9. That is, the
average (mean) reading score for students should be 3rd grade, 9th month.

By applying the single discrepancy analysis, we can see that example A reveals a reading problem. With an average I.Q. score at the national norm, the students here *should*
show reading proficiency at the same norm. Thus reading achievement should be about
3.9 rather than 3.5—a −.4 difference, which represents a significant lag. Example B also
shows a discrepancy in that its slightly higher I.Q. average of 105 should correlate with a
slightly higher-than-average reading score above 3.9. Again, the difference is probably
enough to cause concern, and should be investigated.

Example C probably does not illustrate a reading problem because the above-average
achievement matches the above-average intelligence range. This does *not* mean that
there cannot be a reading problem for certain students in the group. However, both the
average and above-average students are apparently achieving. Example D might also be
reflecting a reading level commensurate with the I.Q. level of its students. This is, of
course, a very rough analysis and does not consider a host of variables, including time of
testing, testing conditions, test validity, types of students, and so forth.

Although it has been widely accepted that minority children and/or children of low
socioeconomic backgrounds do not score well on reading and I.Q. tests, this does *not*
negate the use of standardized test data. This is because if there *were,* in fact, a negative
test bias, such students would score *lower* than their potential on both tests. Therefore,
schools with a disproportionate number of these students must assume that their students can score significantly higher. It should not be assumed that low test scores are an
indication of the potential of these students.

A more workable procedure for determining reading expectancy levels and program
effects in these cases is the use of ideographic analysis. Rapp and Haggart (1) assume
that a student's pretest score represents the average rate of gain he or she has made
during previous years in school. That is, if a sixth grader scores 3.0 at the beginning of
the year, this score, divided by the number of years in school, 6 (assuming the child had
kindergarten and the expected score on entering the first grade is 1.0), equals .5. Thus
the child's average gain per year has been five months. We can expect that, with no
special program, the student will make a five-months gain, on the average, the next

Table 3–3: Reading Scores Compared to I.Q.

	AVERAGE READING ACHIEVEMENT	AVERAGE I.Q.
School or Classroom A:	3.5	100
School or Classroom B:	3.7	105
School or Classroom C:	4.2	110
School or Classroom D:	3.7	90

year. If the gain at the end of that year is 1.0, we can then assume that the additional gain—.5—was caused by increased services provided. Rapp and Haggart caution against using this analysis in the primary grades because there would not be sufficient opportunity for variations in learning rate to average out.

By noting the expected gain versus the actual gain for each student, it is easy to determine which students are performing according to prediction. As we have mentioned, ideographic analysis is appropriate for schools with a high proportion of low-achieving students.

LISTENING AND STANDARDIZED
READING TEST SCORES

Another approach uses a listening test score as compared to an achievement test score as an indicator, because students should be able to read and achieve at about the same level at which they listen and comprehend. This applies particularly to the intermediate grades. At the primary level, especially in grade one, listening scores are higher than reading achievement scores, but tend to equalize by about grade 6 (1).

All of the methods we have discussed will yield only a general indication of a reading problem. By following one or more of these procedures, the principal can at least localize the problem in a particular class or level. A more refined approach, however, is needed to discover precisely where a problem lies.

Reading Achievement Analysis: A Closer Look

A more sophisticated method of analyzing a reading discrepancy involves the use of learning expectancy formulas. This approach depends on the availability of intelligence scores, which, although criticized, are still the best predictors of academic success. If intelligence scores are not available, then alternatives such as the Durrell-Brassard Listening-Reading Test (3) or the Analysis of Learning Potential Test (ALP) can be used (4). Regardless of the test used, it will never be known if the score is measuring a student's true potential. Nevertheless, educators work with the methods at hand until better ones appear.

LEARNING EXPECTANCY LEVEL

The learning expectancy level (LEL) is a formula [MA (Mental Age) − 5 = LEL] developed by Kaluger and Kolson (5) to determine if a student is reading at a level one could reasonably expect. All other factors being equal, the formula yields an estimated potential rather than an absolute score. Other reading authorities have developed expectancy formulas, (for example, Bond-Tinker (6), Myklebust (7), and Harris and Sipay (8)) for the same purpose. The intent of these formulas is not to label children or to place them in a track system, but to determine if, in fact, a reading discrepancy exists. Luty's research (9) compared popular expectancy formulas at the third- and sixth-grade levels for students taking the same reading and mathematics tests. The correlation between predicted and actual achievement was highest (.91) for the Kaluger-Kolson formula. The Bond-Tinker formula had the second highest correlation (.90).

The main criticism of expectancy formulas is that the standardized tests with which they are compared have questionable validity and limited numerical precision because

Figure 3–2:   Sample Computation of LEL

I.O. × CA	= MA – 5	= (LEL)
I.O. × CA (yr./mo.)	= MA (yr./mo.) – 5	= LEL (gr./mo.)
93 × 8.25	= 7.7 – 5	= 2.7

of certain variances. (The standard error for these tests does not allow for a precise numerical evaluation.) Consequently, predicting an (LEL) from two standardized tests can result in its numerical unreliability. Principals must be sensitive to this criticism, but the intent of the procedure is to detect potential problems, not to conduct precision research.

By computing an LEL (there are mental-age charts available from psychological testing firms to make this a simple operation) for each student, one can arrive at an index for a class, grade level, and school. A sample computation is provided above (10).

FINDING A CHILD'S LEARNING EXPECTANCY LEVEL

When using this formula to find a child's potential level, state the chronological age (CA) in years and months (for example, 8 years, 3 months) at the time of the achievement test. The learning expectancy level is also reported in years and months.

Once the LEL has been computed and a discrepancy between the LEL and the achievement test score with which it is contrasted is apparent, one must decide if the discrepancy is substantial enough to warrant serious concern. Because the achievement test scores used are not absolute scores (there is an error of test measurement), some interpretation of the results is needed. The table below is a general guide for determining the possible significance of the discrepancy. The table is based on the premise that the younger the child is, the smaller the discrepancy need be to be considered significant (11). That is, a three-month discrepancy in the fifth grade is not so critical as a three-month discrepancy in the second grade.

Table 3–4

Student in Grade or Level	Difference of
2	3 months or more
3	4 months or more
4	6 months or more
5	8 months or more
6	1 year or more
7–9	1 1/2 years or more
10–12	2 years or more

Intervals at Which Differences Between LEL and Performance Level Determined by Achievement Tests Can Be Considered Significant

Consider the list of students below and their performance levels and computed LELs.

Table 3–5: Student Performance Levels and LELs

Student	Grade	M.A. − 5	LEL	Actual Performance Level as Determined by Achievement Test	Discrepancy
A	5	10.2 − 5	5.2	3.1	− 2.1
B	6	12.6 − 5	7.6	6.0	− 1.6
C	3	8.5 − 5	3.5	3.7	+ 0.2
D	8	13.9 − 5	8.9	7.8	− 1.1
E	12	14.0 − 5	9.0	8.5	− 0.5

It can be seen that Student A has a reading problem, because there is a difference of more than 8 months between his actual performance and his expected level of performance. Student B might also have a problem, because there is more than one year's difference between the two performance levels. Student C is performing as expected—at grade level. Student D, reading below grade level, could use some additional instruction. However, this student probably does not have a serious reading problem because the difference between performance and expected levels is not more than 1.5 years, the point at which the difference would be significant (see Discrepancy Table above). Student E is reading at the expected level, although significantly below grade-level placement.

Assuming that the I.Q. scores are accurate, and using a reading pre and posttest, one could observe changes from September to June by recomputing the LEL at the end of the year. You cannot simply add on nine months, however, because students with low I.Q.'s are not expected to gain 9 months, whereas students with high I.Q.'s are expected to gain more than 9 months.

The severity of a reading problem can also be determined by counting the number of students who scored six months, one, two, or more years below their LELs. If the principal has used an LEL or some similar device, she or he can then chart the percentage of students with low LELs by classrooms and grade level

By preparing similar graphs for each grade at the end of the year, a principal can have visual records of where reading problems exist in the classrooms.

You can also extend the procedure into a system for determining if a reading problem exists school-wide, regardless of where the school stands when its scores are compared to national norms. A school with high test scores may have a reading problem just as much as a school with low test scores. It is not a question of high or low reading scores per se. It is, rather, a question of comparing what the scores *are* to what the scores *should be*.

TREND ANALYSIS

You can chart LEL data for the entire school or at critical grade levels. Such an analysis of the third and sixth grades gives a picture of the performance for a school. If these data are charted over a period of years, trends begin to emerge that are valuable in monitoring progress and identifying problems.

Figure 3–3: Percentage of Grade 4 Students
Reading 6 Months Below LEL

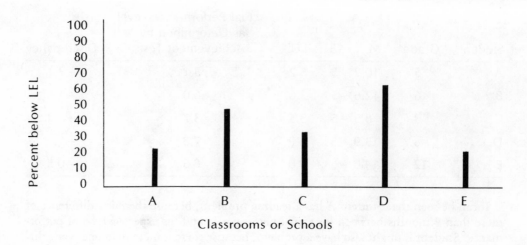

Figure 3–4: Percentage of Grade 3 Students
Reading 4 Months Below LEL

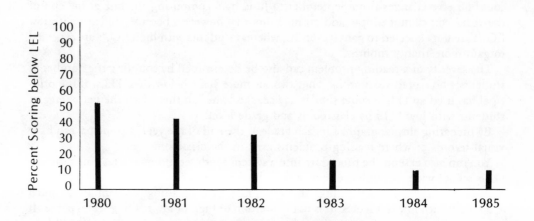

USING THE COMPUTER

If a research department and a computer are available, then the principal can make a more comprehensive analysis. The computer can be programmed to compute LELs for any purpose desired. Through a multiple regression analysis, the effect of such variables as mobility, sex, and socioeconomic level can be used to predict a more reliable expectancy level.

This kind of analysis, advocated by DeGracie and Vicino (12), is used in the Mesa Public Schools in Mesa, Arizona. The data are shared with principals who then set management and instruction program objectives for the coming year. Principals then meet with teachers for problem resolution and for setting classroom program objectives. This process is repeated annually and monitored closely.

SUBSKILL ANALYSIS: DIAGNOSTIC CRITERION-REFERENCED TEST

Many school districts pre and posttest by using criterion-referenced tests that measure mastery of reading objectives. This is very useful in identifying specific problems. It is one thing to know that the first grade has a reading problem, another thing to know that the problem lies in the area of decoding, but something quite special to know which specific decoding skills constitute that problem.

A useful chart for recording criterion-referenced test results for problem identification follows. These kinds of data are also helpful in identifying inservice needs for the staff and specific teachers. In addition, it is important that teachers keep records of pupil progess that can be reviewed by the principal and used as the basis of teacher monitoring and evaluation.

Figure 3-5: Diagnostic Reading Assessment

FIRST GRADE

SCHOOL _____

DATE _____

SKILLS	Dist Avg.	Sch. Avg.	Teachers				
			1	2	3	4	5
Initial Consonant Sounds	95	99	100	96	100		
Initial Diagraph Sounds	92	91	*83	96	92		
Blends	77	76	*54	92	80		
Final Consonants	90	89	*79	100	88		
Final Digraphs	82	76*	*38	92	96		
Short Vowel Phonograms	91	97	100	100	92		
Long Vowel Phonograms	91	85*	*58	100	96		
Sight Words	93	86*	*63	96	100		
Substituting Init. Cons. Sounds	94	93	*88	96	96		
Substituting Init. Dig. Sounds	82	84	83	84	84		
Substituting Initial Blends	78	76	*46	88	92		
Short Vowel Sounds	85	93	*83	96	100		
Long Vowel Sounds	91	91	*75	96	100		
Compound Words	90	95	96	96	92		
Word Endings	69	72	*46	80	88		
Classifying	92	92	*83	96	96		
Context Clues	91	85*	*67	92	96		
Main Idea	77	70*	*63	72	76		
Oral Directions							

Class by Item 85. 96. 96   Class by Objective 69. 88. 88

School by Item   92%   School by Objective   81%

District by Item   92.7%   District by Objective   81.9%

School average starred if 5% points below district average

Teacher average starred if 5% points below school average

5/78

The principal is responsible for using whatever data available to assess the effectiveness of the reading program. However, the importance of this undertaking is not simply to evaluate or predict—although this must certainly be done—but also to provide valuable information that can be used in conjunction with other data to set goals and resolve problems. Such vital data should be used for problem identification and program improvement, not merely as the basis of a report on school performance.

REFERENCES

1. M. L. Rapp and S. A. Haggart, *Ideographic Analysis of Achievement Measures.* Santa Monica, California: Rand Corp., August, 1972. pp. 2–10.

2. Donald D. Durrell, "Listening Comprehension versus Reading Comprehension," *Journal of Reading,* Vol. 12, (March, 1969), p. 457.

3. Donald Durrell and Mary B. Brassard, *Manual for Listening and Reading Tests.* New York: Harcourt, Brace and World, 1969.

4. W. N. Durost, Eric F. Gardner, and Richard Madden, *Analysis of Learning Potential.* New York: Harcourt, Brace and World, 1970.

5. George Kaluger and Clifford J. Kolson, *Reading and Learning Disabilities.* Columbus: Charles E. Merrill, 1969.

6. Guy L. Bond and Miles A. Tinker, *Reading Difficulties: Their Diagnosis and Correction.* New York: Appleton-Century-Crofts, 1979, p. 78.

7. Helmer R. Myklebust, *Progress in Learning Disabilities,* Ed. Vol. 1. New York: Grune and Stratton, 1968.

8. Albert J. Harris and Edward R. Sipay, *How to Increase Reading Ability.* New York: David McKay, 1975.

9. Elanny T. Luty, "A Study of the Validity of Using Expectancy Criteria as a Basis for Accountability," Ph.D. dissertation, Arizona State University, 1971.

10. George Kaluger and Clifford J. Kolson, op. cit., p. 127.

11. Guy L. Bond and Miles A. Tinker, op. cit., p. 76.

12. James S. DeGracie and Frank L. Vicino, "A New Yardstick for Comparing Achievement in Basic Skills," presented at AERA Annual Meeting, Montreal, Canada, April, 1977.

4: What Test Data Won't Tell the Principal

There are elements other than the quality of instruction that tend to affect reading achievement in schools. Although it is difficult to account for the following variables, they do need to be scrutinized when reading achievement is lower than expected. Some of the more important of these factors are

1. staff stability,

2. misuse of materials,

3. inadequate libraries,

4. ineffective kindergarten programs,

5. lack of an early prevention program,

6. poor use of the reading specialist, and

7. failure to preserve instructional time.

Staff Stability

Teacher stability influences achievement, especially at grades one and two. Teachers need the opportunity to develop or master a program at a particular grade level. Since first grade reading instruction is so critical for students, it is neither the place for an inexperienced teacher to learn the craft nor a grade where teacher turnover should be encouraged. Reading achievement is enhanced when competent teachers, knowledgeable in reading instruction, remain at the primary level long enough to develop a sound program.

Longitudinal studies by Kraus (1) and Hopkins (2) suggest that how well a student reads at the third-grade level is a good prediction of how well he will read at the end of the twelfth grade. As Benjamin Bloom states:

> The absolute scale of vocabulary development and longitudinal studies of educational achievement indicate that approximately 50% of general achievement at grade

12 (age 18) has been reached by the end of grade 3 (age 9). This suggests the great importance of the first few years of school—these are the years in which general learning patterns develop most rapidly, and failure to develop appropriate achievement and learning in these years is likely to lead to continual failure or near failure throughout the remainder of the individual's school career (3).

Misuse of Materials

The old cliche that good reading teachers can teach reading from the phone book is just so much verbiage. Students who can learn from such limited sources would probably learn to read even without a teacher. Some bright students *do* learn to read regardless of the quality of materials; however, for most students, the proper use of materials is crucial. This is particularly true for grades one and two.

The most common misuse of basal programs is advancing students to the next book before they have mastered their current one. Teachers need to assure student mastery before moving on to the next level of the reading program. It is common for children to complete required material at their grade level, but show, when tested for placement the succeeding fall, that they need to repeat the materials they had supposedly finished (11). This shows clearly that such students have not mastered the previous level, probably because they did not receive enough practice and reinforcement. Thus it is important to use basal unit tests or school-developed tests to demonstrate student mastery.

Although a school may have a core basal reader system, some teachers leave these books on the shelf and use other approaches, or revert to their "old favorites." Such practices can cause problems for some children, because reading systems differ in their skill sequences and vary in the amount and rate of vocabulary introduction. At the next grade level, the teacher may assume that the children have progressed through the core program. If they have not, the placement test ranks them lower in the reading program, and it takes time to establish basic skills not mastered the previous year. This subversion of the basic program, especially at the primary level, tends to retard reading achievement, and it is the student who is forced to adjust. However, it should be the *teacher* who adjusts to the program so that students will enjoy a systematic learning progression.

Another way to misuse materials is by turning the basal program into a library book. A basal system is designed as a teaching vehicle in which skills follow a sequence and activities are developed to insure student success. Teachers who rush students through this system without directed instruction and practice are misusing the materials and performing a disservice to students.

Subverting and bypassing a basal program weakens the effectiveness of the total reading program. It is important that each teacher operate a program consistent with, and integrated into, the school's reading program.

Inadequate Libraries

In addition to the core reading materials, supplemental materials are needed for skill practice, reinforcement, enjoyment, and provision for individual differences. Library or trade books, on the appropriate level, are very important to the development of a reader. A well-supplied library or media center allows students to practice and reinforce reading skills learned in the basal program. The goal of every reading program is to develop the habit of reading for recreation and personal enjoyment. Therefore, a good reading program should be complemented by an up-to-date library.

The American Library Association recommends that a library contain 8,000 to 12,000 volumes, which is equivalent to about 16 to 24 books per child in a school of 500 students (4). But very few elementary school libraries have a collection of this size, and there are schools where a 40 to 1 ratio exists. This can be misleading, however, because many of the books could be old, unattractive, and unappealing to students. The point is that without access to attractive, interesting books, children do not practice reading.

In addition to the school library, there should be a classroom library of interesting materials. Harris suggests that "a good class library should contain at least fifty books" (5). Magazines, newspapers, and how-to-do books should also be available to students.

Reading achievement is enhanced when students have the opportunity to practice. Reading is just like other skills; the more one practices, the better one becomes at it.

Ineffective Kindergarten Programs

Most educators agree that children should be taught when they are ready to learn without undue frustration. Failure to teach appropriate reading related skills in kindergarten may have a negative effect on the achievement patterns of a school. In some schools, kindergarten students ready to advance into reading instruction are not given that opportunity. The rationalization being that there is plenty of time and no need to hurry and possibly create reading problems for the future. This is an assumption for which there are no supporting data.

If improving achievement is the goal, then children ready to begin reading instruction should be provided with the opportunity to do so (6). This is happening in many schools, as pointed out by Chall:

> It has become common practice in public schools to teach a little reading in kindergarten: Letter names, consonant sounds, some sight words, and a pre-primer or two—and a little writing also. Indeed, the available tested evidence, although limited, continues to be stronger for an earlier than later start (7).

The danger of beginning reading instruction in kindergarten lies in attempting to teach children at a level at which they are unable to succeed because they lack the prerequisite skills. Such action constitutes professional negligence and is doomed to fail. However, failure to provide for those ready to learn and possessing the needed skills is also negligence. Exposing a child to more formal reading instruction depends strictly on the individual child (8) and her or his state of readiness.

Reading achievement patterns improve when children are provided with materials and instruction appropriate for their readiness levels. Reading achievement is depressed when kindergarten classrooms do not provide for those ready to begin reading, or when the class is taught as a group and geared to the less able. Preschool programs, parent involvement, and extended-day kindergartens are options to consider for children lacking readiness skills. Early attention to reading needs will contribute "to the reading success of children, [and] it should reduce the need for subsequent remedial reading instruction" (9).

Lack of Early Prevention Programs

Historically, remedial reading activities began at the intermediate grade levels, not at the primary level. However, remedial activities should start in the first grade, thus focusing on the prevention of reading deficiencies. Providing resources for the child and the teacher at the primary level is the key to reducing the percentage of children who score in the lower quartile of the normal achievement curve. It is critical that students have a solid foundation, for the onset of reading problems lies in exposing children to materials they are unable to cope with successfully. Tragically, if a reading problem persists after the third grade, the chances for correcting it and "redeeming" a reader are very slim (10), (11).

As Gilbert B. Schiffman, former supervisor of reading services in Baltimore County, Maryland, and a former National Right-to-Read Director, states:

> Early detection of reading difficulties can increase tenfold a youngster's chance for a successful school career. The longer remediation is deferred, the less promising are the prospects for improvement. Remedial instruction given early in school can salvage four out of five problem students. In later adolescence, only one in ten improve in reading, but the one student who can be helped shows a marked tendency to regress when remedial instruction is stopped (12).

The chances for successful remediation after the third grade are about 35 percent; after the sixth grade, about 10 percent. This is only logical, as Schiffman notes:

> . . . as the non-reader goes through the primary grades, his problems multiply—he cannot solve the problems in arithmetic or social studies, even though he may have the skills to do so, because he cannot read the examination questions. The impression is one of general academic failure (13).

Use of the Reading Specialist

The use of reading specialists has become a common practice during the past decade (14). Historically, reading specialists worked in a remedial capacity with small groups of students, usually at the intermediate grades. Because the specialist's time was spent directly with students, there was little time left for consultation with teachers. Reading achievement patterns did not significantly improve following this format or model, and it became evident that the key to changing a school's reading achievement patterns rested in the improvement of classroom teacher competence, especially at the primary level. It was assumed that reading problems would continue to develop unless energies were directed toward preventing problems in the early stages, and that efforts to improve the competency of a child's regular teacher were more effective than was time spent with a child in remedial instruction.

In a general attempt to increase reading services, reading specialists were given the role of consulting with teachers—in effect, of being helping teachers (15). Otto and Smith stressed that "specialized reading personnel who are assigned to schools should always work as resource persons for the entire school as well as with selected students" (16). Still, some teachers wanted the reading specialist to spend time on remedial efforts with problem readers (17), so a compromise emerged, dividing the role into that of resource teacher for half the day, with the other half spent working directly with students. The present trend, however, is for the reading specialist to serve as a resource or helping teacher, and not to assume a split role or that of a remedial specialist working directly with students.

Thus the task of the reading specialist evolved from working directly with students to serving as a resource person with responsibility at two or more schools. This trend will almost certainly continue because of economic factors; there is simply no escaping the budget realities of the day. Therefore, the most efficient and effective use of expertise has to be in working with teachers. Clearly, helping the teacher to learn and adapt prevents more reading problems than a specialist can salvage later.

THE EFFECTIVE RESOURCE TEACHER

How the reading specialist functions depends on the philosophy of the school district and on the interpersonal dynamics of the school served. To be an effective resource teacher, a person must have interpersonal skills, recognized content expertise, and the ability to function in a nonthreatening manner. Usually, it takes two years for a resource teacher to build staff trust to the point where teachers realize that the resource teacher is indeed a helping teacher, not someone who serves only to criticize or evaluate others.

SERVICES PROVIDED BY THE RESOURCE TEACHER

For Teachers:

• Helps administer diagnostic and criterion-referenced tests

• Diagnoses individual student needs

• Prescribes appropriate reading instruction

• Evaluates new instructional materials

• Demonstrates new materials and techniques

• Develops needed special materials

• Provides clinical services for severe reading disability cases

• Reports and shares research findings

• Trains and supervises reading paraprofessionals

• Helps order reading materials

• Helps organize and manage classroom

• Conducts inservice workshops

For Administrators:

• Informs administrators of services provided for the school

• Consults and makes recommendations on materials and programs

• Analyzes and interprets reading test data

• Helps meet joint goals and objectives

- Helps identify reading problems and solutions
- Reports and shares research findings
- Helps order reading materials
- Demonstrates new materials and techniques
- Helps organize and manage classroom
- Trains new teachers in the school reading program
- Conducts inservice workshops

For the Community:

- Conducts workshops for parents
- Consults on individual cases
- Provides information on purpose and progress of the reading program

The following chart shows the characteristics of effective resource teachers.

Ten Characteristics of an Effective
Reading Resource Teacher (RRT)

1. The RRT is a professional, never gossips about teachers to others, is never drawn into teacher evaluations (this is not part of the job), is fair and bussinesslike with everyone.

2. The RRT is a teacher, demonstrates new techniques and materials, and asks teachers to use their classrooms to try new approaches.

3. The RRT has a smile, (no one enjoys a sourpuss), is friendly, respectful, and honest while performing his or her duties.

4. The RRT listens, realizes that other people have ideas, biases, and feelings that should be respected, does not have "the answer" for everything, but helps people define and remove problems.

5. The RRT systematically analyzes problems, does not jump to *solutions before* problems are clearly defined, and provides ALTERNATIVES to most recommendations.

6. The RRT is visible (he or she can't be of assistance if never seen), is at assigned schools every day, and is available to help meet day-to-day teacher needs.

7. The RRT has a positive approach, (negative people are seldom accepted by anyone), and emphasizes what can be done, as opposed to giving all the reasons why something will not work.

8. The RRT is adaptive, and can adjust to teachers and principals with different philosophies and needs.

9. The RRT is sensitive to public opinion, is aware of the importance of a public image, and works to project an image of sincerity, competence, and efficiency.

10. The RRT is involved—with students, teachers, parents, and administrators—because that is what she or he desires to do for personal satisfaction.

Preservation of Instructional Time

Students will not become skilled readers unless they have the time to learn and practice. As curriculum demands and special programs increase, time becomes a scarce resource. Students are out of the classroom more often, attending programs such as Title I, bilingual education, music, art, band, and physical education. This often results in decreased time for instruction and practice in reading.

Reading achievement improves when students spend more time actively engaged in directed instruction. It is not time per se that is so critical, but rather more active learning time (ALT). As Noli notes in describing her experiences in implementing this concept in her school, "As one increases ALT, there is, as a result, more content covered. If more content is not covered, increasing time will have little effect on achievement" (18).

In one district, principals have requested 1.5 hours of uninterrupted classroom time. During this time, students cannot leave the classroom for any other program. All special services and programs must schedule around this uninterrupted time frame, which usually varies by grade. It is during this time that basics are taught.

The use of films and special classroom projects can be abused and can also result in a loss of instructional time. Some teachers use an unreasonable number of films, and there are even instances in which films have been shown all morning, sometimes over and over, and sometimes played backwards for amusement! Consider the fact that if films are shown one day a week, (usually on Fridays,) one-fifth of the instructional time for the entire *year* for some subjects is taken away from directed instruction. It is the principal's responsibility to meet with teachers to set guidelines and practices to manage the use of films.

Some teachers also spend far too much time on special projects, such as conducting an art show, making a film, or producing a play. These experiences do have value, but the difficulty arises in the amount of time allotted to these activities. Mornings, when students are as fresh as they will be all day, should be spent on the basics, and especially on reading. Activities should occur toward the end of the school day or when other work is completed.

There are other time-related issues that are best assessed when monitoring individual classrooms—for example, discipline, misuse of seatwork, inappropriately-assigned tasks, and poor organization of material and planning of transition time between lessons. These topics will be treated in later chapters.

REFERENCES

1. Philip E. Kraus, *Yesterday's Children: A Longitudinal Study of Children from Kindergarten into the Adult Years.* New York: John Wiley & Sons, 1973.

2. Kenneth D. Hopkins, "A Longitudinal Study of Constancy of Reading Performance: Grades One Through Eleven," *IRI Annual Convention Abstract,* Newark, Delaware: May, 1970, pp. 41–42.

3. Benjamin S. Bloom, "Stability and Change in Human Characteristics," unpublished paper, n. d., p. 5.

4. American Library Association of School Librarians, ALA, and Association for Educational Communications and Technology, *Media Programs: District and School.* Chicago: American Association of School Librarians, 1975, p. 70.

5. Albert J. Harris and Edward R. Sipay, *How to Increase Reading Ability.* New York: David McKay, 1975, p. 528.

6. Dolores Durkin, "Beginning Reading: When and with What Materials," in *Children Can Learn to Read: But How?* Ed. Morrison Coleman. *Rhode Island College Reading Conference Proceedings.* Providence: Rhode Island College, 1964, pp. 7-16.

7. Jeanne Chall, *Reading 1967-1977: A Decade of Change and Promise.* Bloomington: Phi Delta Kappa, 1977, pp. 14-15.

8. Albert J. Harris and Edward R. Sipay, op. cit., p. 51.

9. U. S. Department of Health, Education, and Welfare/National Institute of Education, PREP Brief, *Preschool Reading Instruction: Information for the Administrator.* Washington, D.C.: U. S. Government Printing Office, number 39, n. d.

10. Phillip E. Kraus, op. cit.

11. Kenneth D. Hopkins, op. cit.

12. Gilbert B. Schiffman, paper presented at the American Association of School Administrators, quoted by *Globe Language Arts Bulletin,* issued periodically, New York: n. d.

13. Ibid.

14. "Right to Read, Reading Specialists: Their Roles Are Changing." Newark: International Reading Association, Vol. 3, No. 2, (December, 1976).

15. Pauline S. Rauh, "Helping Teacher: A Model for Staff Development," *Teachers College Record,* Vol. 80, No. 1, (September, 1978), pp. 157-171.

16. Wayne Otto and Richard J. Smith, *Administering the School Reading Program.* Boston: Houghton Mifflin, 1970, p. 162.

17. John J. Pikulski and Elliott Ross, "Classroom Teacher's Perceptions of the Role of the Reading Specialist," *Journal of Reading,* (November, 1979), pp. 126-135.

18. Pamala Noli, "A Principal Implements BTES," *Beginning Teacher Evaluation Study News-letter No. 5,* (November, 1979), p. 10.

5: Assessing and Monitoring the Classroom Reading Program

Great teaching is an art, good teaching is a science, and poor teaching is unacceptable. One cannot dissociate good reading instruction from good instruction in general. A good reading teacher is not just a good teacher. Before focusing on specific reading instruction, the principal must assess a teacher's expertise in effective climate and classroom management.

This chapter reviews the literature to substantiate the importance of these two areas, and suggests a checklist for initial assessment. Finally, this chapter focuses on the critical instructional management skills directly related to reading achievement and provides a means for determining the presence or absence of these factors.

Affective Climate Management

No behaviors influencing achievement recur more often in the literature than those dealing with the affective climate of the classroom. Most important are enthusiasm, warmth, and expectations communicated by the teacher. These affective qualities alone will not improve achievement, but without them, achievement may be lessened.

ENTHUSIASM

Rosenshine has extensively reviewed enthusiastic teaching as an instructional variable and found it to be positively correlated with pupil achievement (1). Teachers identified as enthusiastic were animated, mobile, energetic, and stimulating. They tended to use more movement, gesture, eye contact, and variation in their voices. The relationship between enthusiastic teaching and achievement rests on the assumption that these teacher behavior patterns keep pupils attentive, and on the task.

WARMTH

Warmth is a characteristic that also enhances achievement. Warm teachers express approval, acceptance, and support, and they tend to speak well of their pupils and people in general (2). Mohan has summarized some of the ways we can tell warmth is lacking:

> . . . a teacher who 1) is blatantly nervous during face to face contact; 2) lacks a strong self concept; 3) does not believe children are capable of loving him and that he can get love from them; 4) is disconnected from his own desires, emotions, and inner experiences, 5) does not release his emotions, 6) is not having contact with his inner self, will find it extremely difficult to create a climate of warmth, affection, and acceptance (3).

Harootunian cites three standardized instruments that can be used more objectively to identify warmth in teachers, although this is an elusive characteristic to define. These are Flanders' System of Interaction Attitude Inventory, the California F Scale, and Ryan's Teacher Characteristics Schedule (4).

EXPECTATIONS

Students will achieve excellence if we expect them to do so and communicate our expectations. The research substantiating the influence of teacher expectations extends beyond the classic-but-controversial "Pygmalion" study (5). As Edmonds states in his review of the research on effective schools,

> There is a clear contrast in the evaluations that teachers and principals make of the students in the improving and declining schools. The staffs of the improving schools tend to believe that all of their students can master the basic objectives; and furthermore, the teachers perceive that the principal shares this belief. They tend to report higher and increasing levels of student ability, while declining school teachers project the belief that students' ability levels are low, and therefore, they cannot master even these objectives. (6).

This was further substantiated by Harris's review of effective reading instruction, in which he points out that teaching is more likely to be effective when teachers are optimistic about the learning potentials of their pupils and do not allow their perceptions of individual differences to adversely affect pupil morale (7). Expectations can be self-fulfilling prophecies communicated in subtle ways, and good instruction requires a sensitivity to this important affective dimension of the classroom climate. Although these characteristics of affective climate management can be identified and recognized, it is highly questionable if a teacher who lacks them can change significantly.

Student Control

The general classroom environment, both physical and emotional, is the third category of teacher behavior that influences achievement. The key here is the skill to maintain appropriate student conduct that results in increased time on task. Without classroom discipline and appropriate student conduct, effective instruction cannot take place.

The importance of this variable appears in a study conducted in the Philadelphia Public Schools (8) in which reading achievement was higher in larger classrooms. The authors attribute this finding to the more effective discipline found in larger classrooms. Thus we can conclude that discipline may be more critical than class size in influencing reading achievement.

Time on Task

There is substantial evidence that achievement is directly related to time on task (9). It is the authors' position, however, that the quality of the task is as important as the time spent on it, if not more so. Teaching to specific skill needs is critical, but students also need time to practice skills. Teachers must promote on-task behavior as well as use available instructional time effectively. In reviewing the relationship among teacher behavior, time on task, and learning, Brophy states:

> Another basic cluster includes such variables as classroom management skills, student engagement, time on task, and opportunity to learn material. Effective teachers know how to organize and maintain a classroom learning environment that maximizes the time spent engaged in productive activities and minimizes the time lost during transitions, periods of confusion or disruptions that require disciplinary action (10).

The skills involved in achieving good discipline and effective use of time can be learned, and it is the responsibility of the principal to identify both the need for these elements and the resources for appropriate training to achieve them.

Management of Instruction

A positive climate and good intentions alone will not result in achievement; there is also a cognitive dimension to the teaching of reading. Effective reading instruction requires knowledge of, and expertise in, systematic instruction.

In summarizing several recent, large-scale, field-correlational studies of teaching behavior and student learning, Brophy finds a cluster of behaviors associated with better learning (11). These critical aspects of teaching include:

1. teachers having and focusing on academic goals;

2. promoting extensive content coverage and high levels of student involvement;

3. selecting instructional materials related to these goals and actively monitoring student progress;

4. using structured learning activities and including immediate feedback; and

5. creating an environment that is task-oriented but relaxed (12).

Specifically, a teacher must be able to diagnose, to prescribe material and plan appropriate activities, to provide directed instruction, to apply skills, to monitor and evaluate, and to provide feedback to all concerned.

DIAGNOSIS

Diagnosis is the critical task of assessing the entry-level skills of students. The data from the assessments are then analyzed and organized so as to place students in materials at their instructional level. The diagnosis takes two forms for most students: 1) a test for placement in the basal reading program, and 2) a reading subskills test to assess subskill mastery.

Diagnosis for student placement in the developmental basal program is best achieved by an informal reading inventory (IRI) or a placement test provided by the publisher. It is important that the placement instrument selected be based on the actual materials that will be used for instruction. Commercial tests not associated with the instructional materials are not so well suited for student placement as are the instruments provided with the reading program.

The second step in diagnosis is the assessment of subskill mastery. Tests provided by the publisher of the basal system are the best source for subskill analysis because the skills tested are related to the objectives of the reading program. School district or other subskill assessment instruments may be excellent tools, but because they are seldom directly related to a sequential skills development program, they tend to foster isolated drill work. In general, purchase the tests from the publisher, because the materials designed to remedy uncovered weaknesses are provided in the developmental program.

Students significantly below grade level need individual diagnostic analyses by appropriate personnel and placement in materials where they can be successful. Low-achieving students need much more practice and close monitoring to stay on task.

PRESCRIPTION AND PLANNING

Once in possession of the diagnostic data, the teacher should then develop goals and objectives to help the student. These goals and objectives should be shared with the students. Suitable materials and the teacher's plan for the use of these materials must be organized for systematic instruction. Once the need and intent are known, the teacher must plan the actual teaching process he or she will use to help students achieve the intended goal.

DIRECT INSTRUCTION

Ever since the Oregon research on the topic (13), educators have acknowledged the importance of teacher-directed instruction. This has also been confirmed by the Beginning Teacher Evaluation Study, which reports that teaching that provides *more direct instruction to pupils* improves pupil learning (14). The report further states: "It isn't whether a teacher teaches in a group; it is whether such teaching provides direct instruction to pupils" (15).

Direct instruction means guiding the learning of students by securing their attention, presenting what is to be learned, giving examples, modeling, asking students to discriminate and recognize, and providing practice and appropriate feedback. This is the essence of instruction.

APPLICATION

Once students understand a skill, they should apply it and practice it in context. If the instruction has been successful, the student will succeed most of the time when practicing the skill. Students achieve more when given the opportunity to practice the skills being taught, so that the teacher may monitor student progress and provide feedback (16).

MONITORING AND EVALUATING

As students practice a skill, the teacher should monitor and respond to their efforts. This is accomplished by observing and evaluating work being done. By recording students' needs, teachers find it easier to give feedback to all concerned. "Unmonitored seatwork or arrangements that keep pupils waiting for instruction is ineffective" (17).

FEEDBACK

Monitoring allows teachers to praise, to reinforce concepts, and to inform students of their successes. This kind of feedback is positive, and motivates students, whose performance should be recorded for communicating to parents and other interested parties.

Diagnosis, prescription and planning, direct instruction, monitoring, application, and providing feedback all make up a teaching sequence that is repeated, with constant adjustments based on student needs. This sequence embodies what teaching is all about, and omitting steps in the sequence is rarely justified.

Monitoring Classroom Reading Services

Once the school and classroom reading programs are working, the principal's next most critical duty is monitoring the delivery of reading services in the classroom. If this is done consistently, there will be more improvement from this activity than from any other a principal could perform. Therefore, it is important that the principal make specific daily plans, so that the expected crises of an elementary school do not detract from the critical task of monitoring the delivery of the reading program. Monitoring is not a substitute for formal evaluation observations, but rather an adjunct to the teacher evaluation process.

The quality of reading services in the classroom depends on the teacher's awareness of individual needs and upon her or his ability to organize to meet those needs. The teacher must make provisions for 1) different instructional levels, 2) individual rates of progress, 3) special weaknesses, and 4) enrichment.

Therefore, a principal must understand the rationale for grouping, and plan a strategy for monitoring the procedures a teacher follows in meeting student needs.

GROUPING TO MEET STUDENT NEEDS

If a school grade is heterogeneously grouped, reading levels in each classroom will range from grade 1 to grade 6 or 8. The typical intermediate classroom has a range of reading levels of about six years (18). And even if students are homogeneously grouped, they will still have different subskill needs. For example, a student might score 4.0 in vocabulary and 6.0 in comprehension, for an average 5.0 reading level. Another student might score 6.0 in vocabulary and 4.0 in comprehension, and again average 5.0. The reading needs are different even though the two students have the same reading level.

Traditionally, classrooms are organized into three main groups—high, middle, and low. Similarly, most teachers have three reading groups. Rarely can a teacher provide for more than the groups illustrated in Figure 5-1.

The top and middle groups comprise developmental readers. That is, they are functioning well—learning and progressing through the reading program at their respective levels. We may call the low group corrective readers. That is, they rank low and have specific needs that are the responsibility of the classroom teacher. The rate of progress for this low group should be as fast as the students can master the material. This group needs more practice and reinforcement work than does the higher group. The super lows are usually called remedial readers; they are reading significantly below grade level, and should receive any additional services available.

Figure 5-1: Three Reading Groups

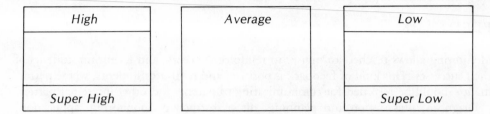

High	Average	Low
Super High		Super Low

The classroom teacher must provide for the needs of these different groups in the time set aside for reading instruction. It is not an easy task, and sometimes the group that is shortchanged the most is the low group. This should not be. If anything, *more* time should be allocated to low groups and *less* time to the top group, which is usually more self-directed. The low group needs not just more time, but increased direct instruction by the teacher. "These students need more monitoring to keep them on task" (19).

ALTERNATIVE GROUPING PLAN

Schools and teachers have devised numerous organizational schemes to better meet the needs of students. The most common method is the three-group plan we have already discussed. An alternative grouping plan is cross-grade grouping, as in the Joplin plan. Here, one or several grade levels may departmentalize for reading, with students changing teachers for the reading period. If a teacher has students at various reading levels in a regular class, it is easier to provide for these differing needs when the departmental plan places only one or two levels in the reading classes. The disadvantage of this arrangement is that the teacher does not really get to know the students so she or he can meet needs in other content areas during the school day. Time is also lost in student movement from room to room. "However, it does come closer to placing each child in a reading situation in which he can experience some success." (20).

After observing this and other organizational plans, we believe that grouping is not critical to achievement. If teachers wish to group students, this is perfectly acceptable, but the crucial element is what happens once the student is in the group. It has been our experience that regardless of the plan, sooner or later teachers end up with a heterogeneous classroom. The question for the principal then becomes, "How can I effectively monitor reading services behind those closed doors?"

Regardless of the grouping options available, at least two basic program components should operate in the classroom consistently. The first component should deliver the basal reading program, and it is discussed in this chapter. The second component should flexibly reinforce specific skills. For this purpose, students are grouped according to subskill needs, usually about twice a week. Students who are not proficient with prefixes, for example, meet together for a short time for direct instruction on prefixes.

PROVISIONS FOR DIFFERENT INSTRUCTIONAL LEVELS

There are two approaches a principal can take in monitoring this area. The first is to ask the teacher how many reading groups are in the class and what criteria are used for placing students in those groups. As we have already said, in a typical classroom there should be a minimum of three basic groups.

The second and easiest method is to visit the room and ask a student to read a paragraph or page to you. Count the number of errors the student makes. If he makes more than three errors per page, he is probably misplaced. As a general rule, a student should make no more than two or three errors per page. If the child reads the page with ease and without errors, you might question the teacher as to whether the student should be placed at a higher level. A student should read on his instructional level, which implies that the text should be neither too easy nor too difficult.

It is very important that students be placed in the reading program at their appropriate instructional levels. To misplace students in the reading program can create frustration or boredom and this cannot be justified. There are basically four reading levels as described below (21).

INDEPENDENT LEVEL	If a child reads approximately 100 words, about 7–10 lines of print, makes no more than 2 errors in word attack, and is able to answer comprehension questions with no more than 1 error, then the chances are that student is reading at his or her independent level.
INSTRUCTIONAL LEVEL	The student can learn at this level and is not frustrated. The child needs some help at this level, but he or she reads with relative ease and fluency. If a child can read about 20 words with no more than 1 error in word cognition, and no more than 2 errors in comprehension, then that student is reading at his or her instructional level.
FRUSTRATION LEVEL	If a child makes more than 1 error every 20 words, reads slowly, and shows signs of stress and frustration, she or he is probably at the frustration level. *No* child should be at this level in the basal reading program.
CAPACITY LEVEL	This is the level at which a student can listen to and understand what is spoken, as evidenced by correct answers to comprehension questions. This provides a rough estimate of the level at which a student might be able to read and comprehend.

*NOTE: For most students, the rule of thumb is that there is 1 grade-level difference between the instructional and independent levels, and 2 grade-level differences between the instructional and frustration levels. If the independent level for Bill Jones is 4th grade, his instructional level will usually be 5th grade, and his frustration level will generally be 7th grade. This is not true in all cases, but usually, once one level is found, the other levels fall within these guidelines.

PROVISIONS FOR INDIVIDUAL PROGRESS RATES

To monitor classroom progress, the teacher can simply fill out the grouping worksheet and summary forms on pages 51 and 52 after students have been placed in the program. This provides the principal with the range of instructional levels within a class.

In late December or in January, teachers should again record the level to which each student is assigned, and complete the classroom summary. By comparing this tally with the one completed in September, the principal can quickly spot teachers who might be going too fast or too slow. Such a record also provides data for the principal to ask specific questions about individual students. The process is then repeated in late spring.

If beginning teachers share a common tendency, it is proceeding too slowly, but teachers who move too quickly through the program present a more severe problem. In this case, students are placed at the next level without mastering the necessary skills. This can be determined by reading the unit test results and by listening to students read and answer comprehension questions to determine if they are, in fact, performing at their correct instructional level.

Figure 5–2: Grouping Worksheet — Ginn

Teacher's Name _____ Grade _____

School _____ Date _____

PUPIL'S NAME	IPT Level	Initial Assigned Level	Mid-Year Assigned Level	Spring Assigned Level	Comments
1.					
2.					
3.					
4.					
5.					
6.					
7.					
8.					
9.					
10.					
11.					
12.					
13.					
14.					
15.					
16.					
17.					
18.					
19.					
20.					
21.					
22.					
23.					
24.					
25.					

Grouping Worksheet — Ginn

PUPIL'S NAME	IPT Level	Initial Assigned Level	Mid-Year Assigned Level	Spring Assigned Level	Comments
26.					
27.					
28.					
29.					
30.					
31.					
32.					
33.					
34.					
35.					
36.					

Class Summary

Reading Level	Initial Assigned Level	Mid-Year Level	Spring Assigned Level
Level 13			
Level 12			
Level 11			
Level 10			
Level 9			
Level 8			
Level 7			
Level 6			
Level 5			
Level 4			
Level 3			

Enter in the columns the number of pupils in the class at each reading level.

PROVISIONS FOR SPECIAL WEAKNESSES

A management or record-keeping system should always be a part of the classroom reading program. Students, regardless of group, will have specific subskill needs. In this case, the principal can choose one or two students in a class and ask the teacher for the specific needs of those students. One might even ask to see the class record chart of skill needs. If the teacher has been keeping records, he should be able to respond with the student's specific, individual skill needs. If the teacher cannot be specific, this probably means that few provisions have been made for special classroom weaknesses.

PROVISIONS FOR ENRICHMENT

A good reading program includes enrichment activities for *all* reading levels, whether in choral reading, dramatics, or social studies. These activities can create interest and motivation, and broaden language experiences. And with such activities, the chances for enrichment increase. If, while observing, the principal sees only work sheets and drill all the time, then provisions for enrichment are probably inadequate.

SCHEDULED CONFERENCES

An effective way to communicate the importance of reading and to monitor programs is to schedule individual teacher conferences at the beginning of the school year and periodically thereafter. At this conference, the teacher can explain the reading program and show how student needs are being met. The teacher should bring to the conference examples of elements of the classroom reading program.

At subsequent conferences, the focus is on the teacher's record-keeping and the progress of specific children. Again, through this process the principal is telling the teacher how important reading is.

Using the program elements discussed in this chapter, the principal and the reading resource teacher may wish to meet with each teacher in the classroom. As questions are asked, the emphasis is on verification. This is a very effective means of monitoring the program, detecting problems, and setting mutual goals for program improvement.

MONITORING THE READING LESSON

The following is a simplified, recommended sequence to follow when teaching a directed basal reading lesson to a group.

I.   Preparing the group for the lesson

    A. Build a background for the new ideas or unknown concepts presented in the story.

    B. Vocabulary development
       a. Present new words on the chalkboard in phrases or sentences.
       b. Analyze new words phonetically.
       c. Analyze new words structurally.
       d. Use the dictionary or glossary where applicable.

II.   Preparing for silent or oral reading

    A. State the purpose(s) for reading the selection by raising a question, giving a problem to solve, and telling the students to read to answer specific questions.

    B. Ask follow-up questions covering different levels of comprehension: main ideas, details, inferences, and critical analyses. Students then read in order to support their answers.

III. Follow up related activities

    A. Provide practice activities related to other language arts. Write a different ending to a story, do an art project, or stage a dramatic scene, etc.

MONITORING SEATWORK

A problem in grouping is what to do with those students who are not in the group and are not being taught at that time. The traditional (and most practical) solution is the often-maligned and misunderstood practice of seatwork. Activities may vary by grade level, but the purpose of seatwork is not to learn a new skill. Rather, it is to practice, apply, and reinforce skills introduced earlier. In some cases, seatwork consists of completing ditto sheets on specific skills or completing workbook activities. The teacher needs these materials for the class to function, and there is nothing *necessarily* bad about dittos. It is the activity *on* the ditto that needs to be examined. If this activity is a ''time-killer,'' then it is a time-waster, and the student is better off doing free reading. If, however, the ditto provides for practice of a skill previously introduced, then the activity has merit *if* the child has not yet mastered that skill. Providing seatwork on skills already mastered results in boredom and negative attitudes.

It is important that students doing seatwork know what they are doing and how it should be done. The principal can circulate around the room and ask students what they are doing, and if they know how to do it in order to learn if instruction has been provided in advance. The teacher needs to prepare and instruct students on the seatwork activities before beginning small group instruction with other students.

There are many excuses administrators can find for not being in the classroom, monitoring the reading program. There is only *one* reason why instructional leaders *do* find the time—the children. The principal is the child's advocate and must insure quality reading services. It is the principal's job.

REFERENCES

1. Borak Rosenshine, ''Enthusiastic Teaching: A Research Review,'' in *Teaching Effectiveness: Its Meaning, Assessment and Improvement,* Eds. Madan Mohan and Robert E. Hull. Englewood Cliffs, New Jersey: Educational Technology Publications, 1975, pp. 105–120.

2. Madan Mohan, ''Specifying Behavioral Components of Some High-Order Concepts of Teaching,'' in Mohan and Hull, loc. cit., pp. 141–153.

3. Ibid., p. 144.

4. Berj Harootunian, ''Research on Teaching Effectiveness,'' in Mohan and Hull, loc. cit., p. 122.

5. Robert Rosenthal and Lenore Jacobson, *Pygmalion in the Classroom.* New York: Holt, Rinehart and Winston, 1968.

6. Ronald Edmonds, "Effective Schools for the Urban Poor," *Educational Leadership,* Vol. 37, No. 1, (October, 1979), p. 18.

7. Albert J. Harris, "The Effective Teacher of Reading Revisited," *The Reading Teacher,* Vol. 33, No. 2, (November, 1979), pp. 138-139.

8. Irwin Farber, Michael H. Kean, Mark J. Raivetz, and Anita A. Summers, *What Works in Reading?* Philadelphia: Office of Research and Evaluation, The School District of Philadelphia, 1979.

9. Carolyn Denham, "The Beginning Teacher Evaluation Study," *The Generator,* Spring, 1979. Also, Joan S. Hyman and S. Alan Cohen, "Learning for Mastery, Ten Conclusions after 15 Years and 3,000 Schools," *Educational Leadership,* (November, 1979), pp. 104-109.

10. Jere Brophy, "Teacher Behavior and Student Learning," *Educational Leadership,* Vol. 37, No. 1, (October, 1979), p. 34.

11. Ibid., pp. 34-35.

12. Ibid., pp. 34-35.

13. Linda B. Stebbins, et al., *Education as Experimentation: A Plan-Variation Model Vol. IV-A. An Evaluation of Follow Through.* Cambridge, Mass.: ABT Associates, April 15, 1977.

14. Frederick J. McDonald, *Beginning Teacher Evaluation Study, Phase II Summary,* Report to National Institute of Education, Washington, D. C., Summer, 1976. Princeton, New Jersey: Educational Testing Service, Summer, 1976, p. 14.

15. Ibid.

16. Ibid., pp. 14-15.

17. Ibid.

18. Albert J. Harris and Edward R. Sipay, *How to Increase Reading Ability.* New York: David McKay, 1975, p. 93.

19. Janet Handler, *Instructional Improvement as a Research Focus,* Practical Application of Research Newsletter, Vol. 1, No. 2. Bloomington, Indiana: Phi Delta Kappa, December, 1978, p. 5.

20. Albert J. Harris and Edward R. Sipay, op. cit., p. 93.

21. E. A. Betts, *Foundation of Reading Instruction.* American Book Company, 1950, p. 448.

6: Effecting Change: The Human Agenda

Improving reading services for children requires change. Program assessment at all levels is vital, but it is only the beginning. Once deficiencies have been identfiied, the real challenge of leadership begins—how to change behavior. The method you use to change a program or classroom will to a great degree determine whether or not you succeed. Many proposed improvements fail not because of their lack of merit, but rather because of the way they are implemented.

People are the critical variable in change. A successful program, practice, or idea requires the motivation of people. They must see the need for change and commit themselves to it, or it will never be realized. This chapter offers a process for implementing change.

The Motivational Process

There are five critical steps in motivating people—in this case teachers—for effective change. They are:

1. Creating an awareness of the need for change

2. Promoting problem "ownership"

3. Generating solutions, selecting goals, and assuming responsibility

4. Evaluating and closing a task

5. Rewarding effort

The basic premise on which this process relies is that unless teachers are "turned on" and motivated, there will not be lasting change. Following is a discussion of each step in this crucial process.

Creating Awareness

Attempting solutions or changes without creating a real awareness of the problem and the need for change is a waste of energy and only results in frustration (2). All too often, attempts at creating awareness become strictly impersonal, cognitive-level approaches using hard data—particularly test scores. In essence, awareness is superimposed, or even worse, mandated, rather than elicited from those directly involved. Data can play an important role when properly used as a means of creating awareness and ownership. Two highly successful awareness strategies are: 1) the use of group consensus, and 2) the use of interviews and information sharing.

GROUP CONSENSUS

You can create awareness by dividing the staff into groups of three to five, depending on staff size, and asking them to list the three critical obstacles preventing them from improving reading services for children. After allowing ten or fifteen minutes, ask each group to present its list in turn and record the comments on a chalkboard, checking those statements repeated by different groups.

By this process, a consensus of opinion and degrees of concern for the key issues are revealed. Do not be surprised if staff concerns differ from the principal's perceived concerns. Nevertheless, these identified problems—the hidden agenda—must be dealt with before one can successfully solve what the principal sees as problems. "People act on what they perceive, and this is what makes the difference" (3).

INDIVIDUAL INTERVIEWS

Another way to create awareness, especially if one is new to a position, is to conduct individual interviews. From these interviews, problems can be identified, tabulated, and presented to the entire staff as the key issues of common concern. Although this is time-consuming, it does afford the principal the opportunity to let each person know that his or her input is valued. There is no more effective process for creating awareness than one-to-one communication.

If time does not permit this approach, an open-ended questionnaire, completed by each staff member, can be used. Some useful questions might include:

1. What are the three most critical problems facing this school?

2. Why are students not achieving at grade level?

3. What do we need to do more of in order to help students?

Essential to either process is that the effort be recognized as a sincere attempt to identify problems from the staff's vantage point. Of equal importance is that you communicate to teachers that *problems* are merely unidentified *goals*. People are not to be blamed for identifying problems but rather assisted in solving them.

Transferring Ownership

Once an awareness had been created that improvements should be made in the reading program, teachers must accept "ownership" of the problems identified and commit themselves to their solution. Often, when a staff is told of a problem, it feels no responsibility for solving it, even though staff members recognize it. The problem must be made personal and moved from an institutional to an individual level. The individual teacher must recognize that since she or he is part of the institution, she or he is also part of the problem. And as part of the problem, she or he must become part of the solution. Accountability necessitates ownership.

The principal begins to implant a sense of ownership by personally questioning the staff at a faculty meeting or through a survey. Some appropriate questions might include:

1. What are we as a school doing about this problem?

2. What am I as an individual doing?

3. What obstacles hinder us from dealing with the problem?

4. Is the problem well-defined?

At this point, a more formal needs assessment is called for. It is also the time to present hard data, especially if they help define the problem or substantiate its existence.

It is important that not too much time elapse between each step of the process, because staff members need to feel that *some* action is underway, and that their involvement is essential to a solution. The principal or leader emphasizes the importance of the task at hand when he makes it a high priority on the agenda and allots it adequate time and resources.

Rarely will any group acknowledge total ownership of a problem. It is important during these early stages to assign the larger, more important tasks to those teachers who demonstrate greater obligation, and lesser tasks to the less committed or more skeptical teachers. Everyone, however, should be involved to some degree. Through this strategy, those who accept ownership are rewarded with the responsibility and recognition that result in self-satisfaction. By assigning lesser tasks to the uncommitted, the principal keeps them involved and not isolated from the activity, as Hostrop explains:

> . . . , the chief problem in overcoming resistance to change lies in the failure to involve those in the solution who are part of the problem. Those who are affected by change *must* participate in that change if the change is not to be sabotaged or to enjoy only a short life (4).

Ignoring or isolating individuals decreases their ownership, commitment, and productivity. A dissenting individual undoubtedly has unmet needs and, rather than isolation from the group, requires consultation, or, if necessary, a reprimand. Giving the individual a small task affords him an opportunity to talk, and thus identify the source of his problem. Nothing solves problems better than face-to-face communication.

Conflict Resolution

Conflict is inevitable in any organization involved in change, and to avoid conflict is to avoid change and the opportunity to improve reading services for children. The challenge is to minimize conflict and use it as a creative force. Likert has noted that " . . .effective organizations are characterized by extraordinary capacity to deal constructively with conflict and resolve it" (5). The effective school and school principal must learn to face conflict and deal with it in a constructive manner.

The first step in resolving conflict is to acknowledge its presence and face it openly. Schutz's simile emphasizes this: " . . . overt discussion is like a cold shower: It is approached with apprehension, the initial impact is very uncomfortable, but the final result justifies the tribulations" (6). This book is based on the assumption that through the sincere involvement of teachers in identifying and solving their own problems, they can create a climate and capacity for resolving conflict.

FORCE FIELD ANALYSIS

Perhaps the most classic and effective technique for facing group problems openly is Force Field Analysis. Jenkins presents a complete explanation of the technique (7). Briefly, its procedure for identifying a problem calls for all participants to list on a sheet of paper all the forces (groups, individuals, and prevalent factors) in the school that can help in achieving the goal or solving the problem. On a second sheet, participants list all the forces that can block the proposed solution or pursuit of the goal. On both sheets, each of the forces is rated in strength from one to ten.

Now, re-examine the two lists, noting which forces on the positive side can be strengthened (and how), and which forces on the negative side can be weakened. List all the options available and prepare an agenda for dealing with them. The important point is that all forces, positive and negative, are stated openly, and that the staff or group is involved in devising the strategies for handling them.

In terms of solutions, Jenkins observes that forces in the field of resistance can be dealt with in only one of three ways, either by 1) reducing or removing the forces; 2) strengthening or adding forces; or 3) changing the direction of the forces. Categorizing the positive and negative forces in terms of these three options helps generate potential solutions (8).

INDIVIDUAL RESISTANCE

Unfortunately, some dissident individuals whose personality or philosophy estranges them from the group may create conflict, and such a situation may represent Shutz's "cold shower." These individuals have needs not met by the process or possible solution, and eventually you must confront their resistance. One hopes they can be neutralized, if not redirected, but their resistance must be addressed face-to-face. Hostrop confirms this:

> The most effective communication process to prevent or resolve conflicts and problems, to give purpose and direction, is through the use of *dyadic* groups (groups of two) . . . Groups of two show markedly *dissimilar* characteristics to *similar* groups of larger size. Dyadic groups are markedly low in showing disagreement and unfriendly behavior, but markedly high on showing tension and asking for information of the others. They appear to take extra care to avoid conflict and to persuade one another gently. [Using] isolated groups of two, . . . frequently resolves mistrust, leads to mutual understanding, and improves the likelihood of goal realizations (9).

There is little question that in confronting resistance the principal must be willing to become part of a dyad with those staff members who impede his efforts to improve the school reading program.

Solutions, Goals, and Responsibilities

Once ownership and commitment to improvement have been established, the natural course of action is to seek solutions to the identified problems. These problems should be stated as goals and clearly understood by everyone involved, because knowledge of group goals enhances their attainment. As Smuck and Runkel state, "Feelings of achievement or self-accomplishment can be harnessed productively when the participants in the organization have a clear conception of one another's goals" (10).

After goal clarification and agreement, the best strategy for arriving at possible solutions is the problem-solving approach (11). Various solutions (and combinations thereof) should be analyzed and the ramifications discussed openly, because they relate to goal achievement.

It is at this point in the process that the group should consider "pet" solutions from staff or others. It is also the best time for using district or outside consultants to offer innovative ideas, to react to solutions, and to explore the advantages and disadvantages of the various solutions under consideration. After all alternatives have been studied, you need to choose a potential solution and state clearly the reasons for its selection.

It is critical, in order to maintain momentum, that the principal accept the staff's selection of a solution, providing it rests within the constraints of available time, space, resources, personnel, and district policy. To solve the problem, ownership for the solution must rest with the teaching staff and not solely with the principal as leader. The responsibility for the solution adds to the staff's sense of importance, and results in its greater effort and higher morale. Its involvement must be real, direct, and significant. The staff must have freedom from, and the support of, the leadership in order to meet its responsibility for implementing the solution. Guidance may be needed, but the staff should feel free to pursue its solution and even to fail, for the only failure that lacks dignity is the failure to try.

Evaluation and Closure

As the staff pursues its solution, whether working in committees or as a total group, it needs to set a timeline, with assessment checkpoints and a terminal evaluation at completion. People need feedback to sustain their efforts and avoid potential problems. Nothing is more demoralizing than to begin a project and never conclude it or have it evaluated. Without formal closure, further attempts to motivate the staff for change will be received negatively with a "why bother" attitude. Too many committees tend to *dissolve* rather than *conclude*.

Rewarding Effort

After the evaluation and closure stages, regardless of the significance of the results, it is highly important that teachers' efforts be rewarded. As McGregor states, ". . . commitment to objectives (and future endeavors) is a function of the rewards associated with their achievement" (12). Effort and achievement must be publicized within the organization and the community. Giving honest praise and recognition of effort shows staff members that the task and time were worthwhile, and that they are valued members of the organization and profession. It also motivates them to undertake future projects and to assume willing responsibility for solving other problems.

Pitfalls

Efforts to promote change may fail for numerous reasons, but the following missteps are guaranteed to demoralize staff, weaken mutual respect, and create mistrust:

1. Nothing discourages people more than predetermined solutions or the feeling that they have been manipulated. This is, in effect, telling staff members that you do not

respect their judgment and that they really are not important. This has a boomerang effect on the principal or leader.

2. Similarly, the principal can impose a solution on a group by using cue words to indicate his obvious wishes. If this occurs, the leader will have accepted ownership of the problem, and motivation will decrease when it is most needed.

3. If the solution and steps of the process are one-way, there will be no commitment or ownership. All decisions should be arrived at jointly, by staff and principal—neither should withdraw from any step of the process.

4. The imposition of unreasonable burdens of time and energy can decrease staff motivation. The principal must show consideration for staff members and for the total scope of their role. Obviously, they have responsibilities and duties besides working on the problem at hand.

In summary, Kirkpatrick defines motivation as "creating a climate in which a person will want to do his best" (13). We believe that the process we have discussed *does* create the type of climate and mutual respect necessary for change to occur. By using these strategies to motivate their staff, and by giving teachers a sense of importance and achievement, principals will find people more willing to try new ideas and go "the extra mile" for success. The significance of this process is that it trains teachers to work as a group in identifying and solving common problems. As their skill and self-confidence increase, teachers begin to believe themselves capable of addressing any challenge—and they will do so. Teacher success ensures leader success; but more importantly, it means greater success for children.

REFERENCES

1. Robert Hetzel and Douglas Barnard, "The Human Agenda: Critical Variable in Innovation," *Educational Leadership*, Vol. 30, No. 6, (March, 1973).

2. Richard W. Hostrop, *Managing Education for Results*. Homewood, Illinois: ETC Publications, 1973, p. 56.

3. Richard L. Foster, "Poise under Pressure," in *Supervision: Emerging Profession*, Ed. Robert R. Leeper. Washington, D. C.: Association for Supervision and Curriculum Development, 1969, p. 17.

4. Richard W. Hostrop, op. cit., p. 56.

5. Rensis Likert, "A Motivational Approach to a Modified Theory of Organization and Management," in *Modern Organization Theory*, Ed. Mason Haire. New York: John Wiley, 1959, p. 204.

6. William Schutz, "Interpersonal Underworld," in *The Planning of Change*, Eds. Warren G. Bennis, Kenneth D. Benne, and Robert Chin. New York: Holt, Rinehart, and Winston, 1961, p. 305.

7. David H. Jenkins, "Force Field Analysis Applied to a School Setting," in Bennis, Benne and Chin, op. cit., pp. 238-244.

8. Ibid.

9. Richard W. Hostrop, op. cit., p. 136.

10. Richard A. Smuck and Phillip J. Runkel, *Organizational Training for a School Faculty*. (Eugene, Oregon: Center for Advanced Study of Educational Administration, 1970), p. 31.

11. Ibid.

12. Douglas McGregor, *The Human Side of Enterprise*. New York: McGraw-Hill, 1960.

13. Donald L. Kirkpatrick, "The Training Managers and Motivation: A Review of Basic Literature," *Educational Technology*, Training Technology Supplement, September, 1969, p. 1.

7: Improving Teacher Competency to Teach Reading

Introduction

Inservice is something that everyone agrees someone else needs. Although past efforts to provide quality inservice training have had limited success (1, 2, 3, 4), most administrators and teachers would agree that inservice training is necessary for, if not essential to, maximizing reading services for students. The dismal history of inservice begs for new approaches and more effective strategies if the goal of improved revitalized teacher competence is ever to be realized.

Negative attitudes expressed toward inservice programs are often caused by poorly-conceived programs lacking planning, and which are too frequently based on faulty assumptions about adult learning. Teachers *do* want to learn and grow, but it is an erroneous assumption that they welcome any and all training. If training is not considered relevant, it will only meet with resistance. Relevance comes when teachers are involved in the total process, from identifying the need for training, through planning the presentation and mode of instruction, to implementing, and finally, to evaluating. Relevant inservice is something done *with* people and not *to* them. To quote Lawrence, " . . .inservice is something done to people for their own good, and the people being done unto don't really have much to say about it" (5).

Inservice programs conceived in the district or principal's office without consideration for creating an awareness of the need for training or the transfer of ownership for that need, will not have an impact on teachers to the benefit of children. Effective inservice comes from communicating the real needs of teachers, in the form of requests for assistance, through the administration to the superintendent. Principals play the key role in eliciting these needs, as well as in collaborating with district staff in helping teachers gain an awareness of the problems that can be solved through inservice training. Teachers and administrators suddenly thrust into inservice training cannot help receiving a subtle message that somehow they are deficient and their performance is poor. The "human agenda" is vital to successful inservice.

Why Have Inservice?

The first question any principal should ask is "Why have an inservice program?" There are five basic answers to this question:

(1) to present new ideas, data, and information;

(2) to change values and attitudes;

(3) to improve the classroom teacher's competence in performing specific tasks;

(4) to motivate teachers; and

(5) to pursue new approaches to problems.

It is essential that the goal of the training be written down and matched with the type of inservice required to meet that goal.

Defining and Diagnosing the Problem

As we have seen, the first step is to determine if a reading problem exists and, if so, whether it can be solved through inservice training. A problem is any discrepancy between what is and what ought to be. It is essential that "what should be" is defined so that you can judge whether a problem exists. This premise assumes that the elements of a reading program are established and are monitored by the principal, or that a process has been introduced to move the staff toward building a school reading program, and that inservice training would facilitate that effort.

Clearly, not all problems can be solved through inservice training. Inadequate materials, philosophical stagnation on the subject of reading, or gross incompetence at any level in the system can impinge on the effectiveness of the reading program, and will not be solved through inservice training. Inservice training is appropriate when an increase in knowledge or skill, or an improvement in attitude would solve the problem. Of these three, increased knowledge and skill are the easiest to deal with successfully through inservice training.

Creating Awareness and Setting Expectations

Everyone recognizes and generally acknowledges the need for continued growth and improvement. The dilemma resides in the discrepancy between what the principal and the individual teachers see as the "needed" areas for growth. The critical link in arriving at a commonly-identified need is effective communication, and, "communication is the act of the receiver" (6). In essence, communication requires the involvement of both senders and receivers. Thus those whom we hope to affect by inservice training must be totally involved in the process of identifying the need and planning the subsequent program.

Evaluation of the reading program, as described in Chapter Three, is an effective way to create an awareness of the need for inservice. The process of gathering and analyzing data is a natural way for the principal and staff to arrive jointly at inservice needs and goals.

Establishing a professional growth committee is also a common approach to creating awareness. The mere existence of such a committee means that the staff agrees that additional training is an inherent part of the profession of teaching. Either through evaluation or a specific charge to meet an identified need, the committee can begin planning an inservice program. The essential element is that the teachers be involved in planning how the program will be conducted and, in particular, how much time will be devoted to it. If they agree that there is a need, they will commit sufficient time. If not, they will undoubtedly propose a more limited program. What is important is that an awareness of the need has been created and the opportunity to express that awareness has been made available.

Surveying Perceived Staff Needs

The most common method of creating awareness is to devise a list of topics and ask teachers to rank them, in order of preference. This procedure limits the topics available and may not include what the teachers really want or feel is needed. It is better to ask teachers to list the topics they would like to have presented for additional training and learning. Logan and Erickson (7) presented a list of suggested training topics to which two hundred teachers responded. Teachers with more experience desired different training than did teachers with less experience. Thus, inservice training should be personal and local if it is to be successful. It is questionable if this approach truly taps critical needs; mostly, it tends to reflect popular topics and only those minimal deficiencies people will acknowledge publicly.

Planning Effective Inservice

Time is the scarcest resource and the single item most prized by the teachers involved. Thus the decision as to who will attend the inservice sessions, and for how long, is of prime importance. There are three basic alternatives for attendance: (1) compulsory—everyone goes for the whole program; (2) voluntary—only those who choose to go attend the program; and (3) by mutual consent—those involved attend as much as they feel is valuable. Remember, time is precious; if certain teachers do not need to be there, they should not attend. And one other critical point should be made: if the principal participates totally, inservice will be seen as more important, and attendance will be less questionable, than if the principal does not participate. In addition, the principal's attendance will build morale and teachers will be more attentive.

The time of day inservice is held is important. Whenever possible, release time should be used for inservice programs. If that is not possible, then the sessions before or after school should be short and highly motivating. Coffee and cookies always ease the acceptance and warm the atmosphere.

People who can lead the program effectively are essential. "Good old boys" and "the lucky one who got to go to the last convention" just may *not* be the people to conduct the program. Mention the presenter's name, and if the staff responds with a groan, get someone else.

Planning inservice with funds is more exciting (and realistic) than proceeding penniless. Too often, inservice training is not budgeted; this places serious limitations on the use of materials and on the quality of trainers. Without a budget even doughnuts and coffee are impossible! It is crucial that the program be designed to take into account the time, space, money, and expertise available.

SELECTING APPROPRIATE ACTIVITIES

The first step is to state clearly the goal of the inservice program. What is to be achieved? Why is it being done? What is the target population? Who will lead the training? What will be the mode of instruction? Table 7–1 helps identify the best available option to meet the particular goal.

Matching the perceived need, mode of instruction, and available resources is a difficult task, and good inservice training requires the same careful planning and consideration as does a good reading lesson

Table 7–1: Factors to Consider in Meeting Inservice Goal

Goal	Attendance	Organization	Leader	Instructional Mode
	Voluntary	Large group	Principal	Slide tape
	Compulsory	Small group	Staff teacher	Film
	Mutual consent	Individual	Planning	Buzz groups
	Individual	Combination	team	Lecture
	growth plan	of above	Film expert	

SETTING EXPECTATIONS FOR THE PRESENTER

If the training is to be done by someone other than the principal, it is essential that the principal or committee representative work closely with the person selected. After explaining the problem and the purpose, both people should discuss the possible means of presenting needs. During the discussion, the principal should ascertain the following:

1. That the presenter understands the problem that prompted the need for the inservice

2. That the presentation will meet the goals and objectives

3. That the presenter can explain his or her approach and activities, and that there is substance to the plan

Evaluation

Following the inservice program, try to determine if the inservice was effective for the purpose intended. Here are some ways to evaluate the effectiveness of inservice training:

1. Administer a written or oral test.

2. Interview participants.

3. Analyze results of test scores or some other product evaluation.

4. Administer a questionnaire.

5. Observe the program.

Although one or more of these techniques can be used, the final judgment might very well be in favor of classroom observation to determine if what was provided in training, is in fact, being incorporated in the classroom experience.

Reassessment

Adjustments should be made at any point in the long-range plans when the sessions are not proving effective. This keeps the program on target and allows for immediate correction. Waiting a long time between evaluation and correction tends to displace the original goal, so it is better to end the training than to subject teachers to a waste of time and energy.

Recognition

After closure and reassessment, the principal should recognize the effort of teachers through expressions of praise and appreciation. During the training, even the small effort of providing refreshments is appreciated by teachers. The presence of the principal throughout the workshop or training session is also rewarding for the staff—and for the principal as well.

A summary of the procedures involved in setting up an inservice program might take the form of Figure 7–1.

Figure 7–1: Checklist for Setting Up Inservice

GOAL	What should be happening in the reading program?
WHAT IS OCCURRING IN THE PROGRAM?	Collection of facts
ASSESSMENT	What is the difference between what *ought* to be and what *is*?
PROBLEM	Is the problem one that inservice will aid? If not—STOP.
ESTABLISH AWARENESS	Present data, conduct group discussions, interview teachers, or just declare the problem and discuss with those closest to the problem the means to change it. A committee could be formed to assist.
SET EXPECTATIONS	Reach agreement on goals, standards, and time.
RESOURCES	Are there resources to do the needed training? Time? People? Space? Money?
PLAN DEVELOPED	Determine content of training and process through monitoring checkpoints.
IMPLEMENTATION	Training program in progress
EVALUATION	Evaluate total process and effect. This brings closure to the effort.
REASSESSMENT	If formative checkpoints are off-target, corrective processes should begin.
RECOGNITION	Praise the staff for its effort and tell others in the district, giving credit to staff and all those who have helped.

Personalized Inservice

Inservice training in most school districts is limited to easily-identified group needs. Rarely is inservice training provided for the teacher who does *not* see the need, nor is training offered for individual professional growth and enrichment.

INSERVICE FOR THE TEACHER WHO DOES NOT SEE THE NEED

As principal, your first step here is to schedule a conference with the teacher to discuss your concern and the discrepancy between what *ought* to be and what *is*, whether it be low test scores or deficient teaching. Once the discrepancy is recognized, the next step is to devise (together) an individual growth plan to solve the problem. The point is to promote teacher growth in a supportive manner. Set an objective and outline a process to encourage growth and to help the teacher succeed. Explain that dates will be set to observe progress toward the objective. A format and record for the conference might look like Figure 7-2 (8).

Figure 7–2: Format for Teacher Growth Plan

GROWTH PLAN FOR _____

Objectives for Growth Plan:

1. _____
   _____

2. _____
   _____

3. _____
   _____

Strategies to Meet Objectives:

1. _____
   _____

2. _____
   _____

3. _____
   _____

4. _____
   _____

Monitoring Dates:

1. Date: _____
2. Date: _____
3. Date: _____

Results:

_____ Objectives achieved

_____ Progress is being made. Continued work is necessary to meet objectives.

_____ Objectives have not been achieved.

Recommendations: _____
_____

NOTE: Strategies might include: 1) visiting another teacher; 2) taking a course; 3) reading a book; 4) interviewing others.

INSERVICE ENRICHMENT

If a school or school system hopes to continue to grow and to meet new challenges, it must provide opportunities for its people to grow with it. A truly personal inservice program meets varing interests, needs, and growth options. These can range from access to an article or literature on a topic to long term, on-going training. In order to meet these different levels of interest, different learning styles, and topics, the following survey chart can help. Topics (culled from a teacher survey or given by a teacher inservice committee) appear in the left column. Teachers can then mark the appropriate column showing their level of interest and commitment to a certain topic. By using these data, you can plan an early release day or develop individual inservice strategies. As each program is completed, teachers are offered the opportunity to pursue the area in more depth if they so desire.

Figure 7–3: Sample Survey

Inservice Topic or Objective	Would like an article or literature	Would like a brief explanation, i.e. an hour lecture	Would like an on-site visit or hands-on experience	Would like an extended or on-going training program
1.				
2.				
3.				
4.				
5.				

Principles of Effective Inservice

The following principles are for your reference in planning effective inservice training.

1. Inservice training, if properly conceived and implemented, reaches all teachers, regardless of their degree of motivation for improvement.

2. Teachers want and need to know the school's ground rules and expectations and how well they are working toward these goals.

3. Personal needs must be satisfied if organizational needs are to be met through inservice.

4. Awareness of a problem and readiness to recognize it must be present if the purpose of inservice is to be fulfilled.

5. Teachers should participate in planning the inservice program. The effectiveness of inservice is a direct function of the amount of activity and participation of teachers.

6. The goal of inservice can be realized only if matched by appropriate instruction and resources.

7. To maximize inservice training, formal evaluation is essential. Summary evaluation helps insure that mistakes will not be repeated.

8. The more attuned is the inservice to the classroom and school, the greater is the potential for achievement. The most effective training is in the classroom and on the job.

9. Remember, it is not so much what you, as a principal, *say* to people, but rather what you have them *do* and how willing you are to *join* them.

Inservice is an on-going process of professional development and, in a sense, it never ends. The purpose of inservice implies more than change; it implies improvement and growth. If services to children are to improve, teachers and administrators must seek new solutions, practices, and ideas. To forgo inservice training is to forgo an opportunity to make a difference in improving services for children.

REFERENCES

1. Wayne Otto and Richard J. Smith, *Administering the School Reading Program*. Boston: Houghton Mifflin, 1970, p. 175.

2. Fred H. Wood and Steven R. Thompson, "Guidelines for Better Staff Development," *Educational Leadership*, Vol. 37, No. 5, (February, 1980,) pp. 374-378.

3. William W. Wilen and Richard Kindsvatter, "Implications of Research for Effective In-Service Education," *The Clearing House*, April, 1978, pp. 392-396.

4. Robert C. McKean and Bob L. Taylor, "News Notes," *Education Leadership*, Vol. 37, No. 2, (November, 1979), p. 189.

5. Gordon Lawrence, "Effective Inservice Education: What the Research Says," *Reporting on Reading*, Right to Read. St. Louis: CMREL, June, 1979, p. 5.

6. Richard W. Hostrop, *Managing Education for Results*. Homewood, Illinois: ETC Publications, 1973, p. 138.

7. John W. Logan and Lawrence Erickson, ''Elementary Teachers' Reading Inservice Preferences,'' *The Reading Teacher*, Vol. 33, No. 3, (December, 1979), pp. 330–334.

8. Adapted from a teacher growth plan used in the Mesa Public Schools, Mesa, Arizona.

8: Selecting Instructional Materials

The one area of reading instruction that could result in greater services to students and decreased financial expenditure, if properly managed, is the selection of appropriate instructional materials. Inadequate processes for selecting reading materials is one of the most critical problems facing schools today (1). Never in the history of education have there been so many basic and supplementary materials to choose from; and never in recent time have budgets been more stringent. There are, in conservative numbers, over 200,000 educational items being marketed to schools today, with new companies being formed regularly (2). The majority of these materials are for reading and the basic skills because publishers realize that these are the areas in which school districts spend their money.

Most educators agree that,

1. There is an abundance of materials in most districts;

2. Many of the supplementary materials are bought because of teacher curiosity and attractive packaging;

3. Teachers are basically unsophisticated in evaluating materials;

4. Teachers should become more proficient in identifying, selecting, and using materials, especially in this era of budget and program accountability.

By improving selection procedures, educators can enhance reading program services and manage budget acquisitions more efficiently.

Selecting the Basic Core Program

Historically, the commonest procedure for selecting basal textbooks has been the formation of a district committee on which all grade levels are represented by one or two faculty members from each school. Using some general guidelines, this group evaluates the various reading systems and recommends its choices to the curriculum director and eventually to the Board of Education. In recent years, parents, and occasionally students, have joined in the process. In some cases, parents even have voting privileges, while in others they serve solely as advisors. *The fact remains that unless districts provide for teacher voting, many of those charged with the responsibility of implementing the selected program have little input or control over which texts are chosen.*

There have been and are alternative processes used by different districts. Some principals simply tell teachers to look over the different reading series and make a recommendation. In some districts, teachers are allowed to buy whatever program they desire under the umbrella of the "eclectic" approach. This "approach" wreaks havoc on continuity, especially for students at the primary level. Both approaches are ineffective.

Some districts use pilot programs with students. This is a logical approach, but it carries several disadvantages and, generally, proves nothing (3). Its main drawback is that a pilot program disrupts continuity for students. When a pilot is done, usually for just one classroom for each level, what happens when those students (especially primary students) enter another system the following year? They encounter differences in vocabulary, rates of vocabulary introduction, syntax patterns and complexity, and in presentation and sequence of skills (4) (5) (6) (7). Pilots are too short and lacking in statistical control to permit any conclusion other than that a teacher may like or dislike the program.

Therefore, we do *not* recommend the pilot method of evaluating reading programs. However, any evaluation process must contain provisions to assure learner verification. Although years ago few materials had this component (2), the most respectable publishing companies now provide verification of the effectiveness of their materials with different types of students.

In the Mesa School District process, after the reading systems choices have been narrowed down to two or three, committee members compose a series of questions to ask users of the system locally or in other parts of the country. School districts using the systems under consideration are identified and visits are planned or phone calls made to the teachers and administrators in those locations. This process informs the district of a program's strengths and weaknesses, including the effectiveness of the consultants who help implement the program.

THE PRINCIPAL'S DIRECTION

Principals must provide leadership in selecting the materials that will best meet the needs of their students. It therefore behooves principals to familiarize themselves with the materials needed in a good program, those currently used by their staffs, and those available on the market. In many districts, the adoption of basic texts is a district responsibility. In such cases, it also behooves the principal to seek advice in the process and to involve teachers.

A PROCESS TO FOLLOW

Any process should ideally involve all teachers, principals, and parents within the area served. Since this is impractical, the next best choice is to form a committee representative of each group, then report to the group represented for advice and consultation in order to assure greater acceptance of the textbooks finally adopted. Committee work usually proves a most efficient process, and, with a few modifications, the majority of each group can be involved and feel ownership. The suggested procedure can be outlined in a task sequence, the critical steps of which follow in figure 8-1.

Figure 8–1: Textbook Evaluation

1.0	Organize Steering Committee	The first step is for the principal to organize a steering committee that will make the major decisions in adopting a basic reading system. This committee should be composed of strong leaders recognized by their peers as being knowledgeable in the field and should include one administrator, a teacher from each grade level, and two parents. The chairperson may be appointed or elected. The principal serves as ex-officio member.
1.1	Establish Philosophy	State the district's or school's reading philosophy given the student population, and make it available to all subcommittees. This is an important program selection criterion.
1.2	Set Operational Plans for Subcommittees	Determine the tasks that need to be completed and the sequence for accomplishing each step. For reading programs, a division of labor is more efficient. That is, one or two people might evaluate all teachers' manuals exclusively, according to predetermined criteria.
1.3	Establish Criteria and Format	Determine criteria and categories to be evaluated, and a way to combine data at the end, so that a decision is possible.
1.4	Select Members Needed to Complete Tasks	Select administrative, parent, and teacher representation for the committee.
1.5	Assign Chair	Make each member of the steering committee the chair of every subcommittee. Therefore, the number of people on the steering committee should match the number of subcommittees. This keeps the strongest and most knowledgeable people in control and assures proper evaluation.
2.0	Meet with All Committees	The second major step is to meet with all steering committee members to set the boundaries, assign tasks, and set time limits and inservice needs by providing specific guidelines and evaluation criteria. The total process is explained to all members.
2.1	Assign Specific Tasks	Each chair meets with each subcommittee and presents tasks decided on by the steering committee.
2.2	Review Criteria	Each chair reviews, adds, deletes, or revises the criteria, and provides inservice on how to evaluate that specific area.

3.0	Narrow Materials to 5–8 Systems	In most cases, there will be about fifteen reading systems presented for adoption. Thus you should narrow the program options to 5–8 systems.
3.1	Evaluate Philosophy and Broad Categories	The philosophy and broad categories from the master form in this chapter (Steps 1.1 and 1.3) must be shared with all subcommittees. Each subcommittee then takes a broad category (committee task) to evaluate for each system, using a 3- or 5-point rating scale.
3.2	Evaluate Scoring	Each subcommittee chair then reports the total points for that category to the steering committee chair, who tallies them on the chalkboard. Low-scoring systems, because of philosophy, readability, or for whatever reason, are eliminated.
4.0	Evaluate Materials	Teachers should be released from class to attend the first all-day work session. Reemphasize the process for using criteria sheets. The subcommittees then begin to evaluate the five to eight reading systems for the category assigned to them.
4.1	Complete First Subcommittee Evaluation	Provide initial evaluation report to the steering committee chair.
4.2	Complete Second Subcommittee Evaluation	If time permits, validate the evaluation. To validate reliability after the first evaluation, each subcommittee member changes committees and evaluates another section or category. A report is provided to the steering committee chairperson. If the two subcommittees agree, it is a valid evaluation.
5.0	Steering Committee Reconvenes	Tabulate all data from subcommittees for each reading system. If there is a large discrepancy among subcommittee reports on the same category, the steering committee should reevaluate that category.
5.1	Analyze Data	Analyze, summarize, and put all data into a presentable form.
5.2	Share Results	Share evaluation results with all subcommittee members. Devise questions to clarify points of concern.

6.0	Invite Publishers to Present Programs Being Considered	At this presentation, the publishers have an opportunity to present their program. Another purpose is to ask questions raised during step 5.2. Subcommittee members hear the presentation, ask questions, and then meet to discuss any changes in their evaluation they deem appropriate. All principals, teachers, and parents should be invited to hear these presentations.
7.0	Reconvene Steering Committee	Final tabulations are completed and programs are narrowed to two or three.
8.0	Steering Committee Verification	The steering committee develops a set of questions to ask actual users of the program. It then visits schools using the program and talks with teachers, or it phones schools in other locations. A point system is devised for each question so results can be tabulated. In addition, verification data are requested from the publisher for additional information.
9.0	Community-Teacher Involvement	While verification is taking place, samples of the 2–3 reading systems are placed at individual schools and/or central locations within the district, along with a one-page evaluation form. Parents, teachers on the committee, and staff are invited to examine the books, fill out the evaluation form, (Figure 8-2, immediately following) and send it to the steering committee chair. These results are tabulated and considered as a separate category, because this evaluation is superficial, unlike that done by the subcommittees.
10.0	Reconvene Steering Committee	The steering committee considers 1) the original evaluation, 2) verification data, and 3) the teacher-parent input and makes a decision. The reasons why one reading program is selected over another should be documented.
11.0	Presentation to Board of Education	The reading program selected is presented to the Board of Education for district adoption.

Figure 8–2: Reading Adoption Survey

DIRECTIONS:
1. Please write the school you represent _____
2. Indicate the grade level you teach (teachers only) _____
3. Put a check mark if you are a parent and not a teacher or administrator _____
4. Please examine the three series and then respond to each statement below for each series of textbooks being considered.

	TEXTBOOK SERIES								
CRITERIA	**1**			**2**			**3**		
	Low		_High_	_Low_		_High_	_Low_		_High_
1. The durability of the textbooks—how well will they hold up with student use.	1	2	3	1	2	3	1	2	3
2. The size of print is appropriate for the grade level.	1	2	3	1	2	3	1	2	3
3. The scope and sequence match the district scope and sequence.	1	2	3	1	2	3	1	2	3
4. At grade ___ , the number of new words introduced is appropriate.	1	2	3	1	2	3	1	2	3
5. The vocabulary at other grade levels is appropriate.	1	2	3	1	2	3	1	2	3
6. The teacher's manual is clear enough for a substitute to use.	1	2	3	1	2	3	1	2	3
7. The T. M. lesson plan is practical to use with the present class.	1	2	3	1	2	3	1	2	3
8. The vocabulary and comprehension exercises in the workbook match the text.	1	2	3	1	2	3	1	2	3
9. The placement and evaluation tests are thorough and easy to use.	1	2	3	1	2	3	1	2	3
10. The ditto masters reinforce skills taught in lessons.	1	2	3	1	2	3	1	2	3
11. There is a variety of interesting stories for your grade level.	1	2	3	1	2	3	1	2	3
12. The content represents different cultural and ethnic groups.	1	2	3	1	2	3	1	2	3
13. The values in the stories are appropriate for our community.	1	2	3	1	2	3	1	2	3
14. Male and female role models are varied and not stereotyped.	1	2	3	1	2	3	1	2	3
15. The series follows the philosophy stated in the teacher's manual.	1	2	3	1	2	3	1	2	3
16. The series provides specific activities for the more and less able students.	1	2	3	1	2	3	1	2	3

ADDITIONAL COMMENTS: _____

_____

Thank you for taking the time to complete this textbook examination.

CRITERIA FOR EVALUATING A READING PROGRAM

The following criteria can guide your considerations and concerns in evaluating a modern reading program. They will serve their purpose most effectively when they direct the attention of teachers, administrators, and supervisors to the essential features of a program, which determine its instructional value.

An individual school conducting the evaluation can use the same process, only all teachers should participate in the division of labor. Asking one school faculty to evaluate all the reading systems on the market is an overwhelming, if not impossible task.

A school or a small school district can survey larger school districts to determine their top reading systems, then evaluate these in depth, using the following criteria. This is at least a manageable task, and can save a tremendous amount of time and energy.

Figure 8-3: Criteria for Evaluating a Reading Program

The purpose of this checklist is to provide a guide to the considerations and concerns in evaluating a modern reading program.

It will serve its purpose most effectively if it directs the attention of teachers, administrators, and supervisors to the essential features of a program, which combined determine its instructional value.

SUGGESTED RATING PROCEDURES:

After studying each question, record your judgment in the space provided as **O**utstanding, **G**ood, **F**air, or **U**nsatisfactory.

	Series A	Series B	Series C
AUTHORSHIP			
Does the combination of Authorship and Consultants include:			
A. experts whose interests range from basic research to practical classroom techniques in teaching reading?			
B. experienced authors who understand the interests and attitudes of today's youth?			
C. recognized leaders in the field of reading instruction?			
D. educators concerned with balanced portrayal of ethnic groups, handicapped people, minorities, the aging, and social issues such as violence, ethics, and use of language.			
PHILOSOPHY			
Does the program include:			
A. a systematic and sequential development of reading skills?			
1. decoding with meaning			
2. comprehension of ideas			
3. evaluation of the author's message			
4. applying the ideas acquired			
B. an emphasis on achieving early independence in reading?			
C. the development of an appreciation and understanding of good literature?			
D. the opportunity to apply the reading skills to related content materials including life and study skills?			

Criteria for Evaluating a Reading Program

	Series A	Series B	Series C
E. provision for the individual pupil's special interests, abilities, and needs?			
F. a bridge to independent reading by fostering understanding and enjoyment of a variety of content?			
G. an emphasis on comprehension and thinking and reasoning skills through the application of all aspects of the program (decoding vocabulary development, content, life and study skills, etc.)			
H. an introduction to reading skills that will enable pupils to relate what is known to the new?			
CONCEPT LOAD			
A. Is the vocabulary development consistent with the child's natural use of the language?			
B. Is the Word List based on the latest research on the words children know and use?			
C. Are words, sentences, and length of paragraphs appropriate for the level of the program?			
D. Are concepts appropriate to the child's level of development?			
E. Is the introduction of new vocabulary sufficient to enable the student to practice learned decoding skills?			
F. Are vocabulary words thoroughly introduced and understood as facilitating story comprehension and expanding the child's vocabulary?			
G. Are known vocabulary words repeated in stories/units and in practice activities after initial introduction?			
H. Does vocabulary development place emphasis on word meaning to enhance comprehension?			
I. Are the multiple meanings of words explicitly taught so children know that familiar words may be used in various ways?			
CONTENT			
A. Is there a good balance of reading content			
1. between modern writing, children's classics, and the reservoir literature			
2. between reading for entertainment and reading for information?			

Criteria for Evaluating a Reading Program

	Series A	Series B	Series C
3. between realistic and fanciful selections?			
4. between non-fiction and fiction?			
5. between a variety of backgrounds and environments?			
B. Do the selections present a variety of literary forms or genres — drama, poetry, narrative, and non-narrative selections?			
C. Are the selections well written, lively, and appealing to today's youth?			
D. Does the content include long selections to encourage library use?			
E. Are selections organized to stimulate additional study by able students and provide the thematic consistency needed to teach students?			
F. Do the selections provide positive role models of females, handicapped people, and minorities?			
G. Do the selections lead children to apply reading skill to a variety of content areas?			
H. Is the length of the selections appropriate to be read during a class period?			
DECODING			
A. Are skills prioritized and are instruction and practice carefully sequenced so that the child achieves mastery of basic decoding skills?			
B. Are basic decoding skills systematically taught and then applied and maintained?			
C. Is there sufficient instruction on letter-sound correspondence — both consonant and vowel correspondences — in the initial levels of the program?			
D. Is decoding taught in context to enhance meaning?			
E. Are the decoding skills related to the vocabulary taught in the selections?			
F. Is the use of decoding skills encouraged for the achievement of early independence in reading?			

Criteria for Evaluating a Reading Program

	Series A	Series B	Series C
VOCABULARY			
A. Are decoding clues used as a technique of vocabulary development?			
B. Are meaning clues used as a technique of vocabulary development?			
C. Can teachers easily identify new vocabulary to be taught before reading a selection?			
D. Is emphasis placed on both word meanings and word recognition?			
E. Is the relationship of vocabulary to comprehension stressed?			
F. Are strategies for vocabulary development taught?			
COMPREHENSION			
A. Does the program provide for systematic introduction to and instruction in comprehension skills?			
B. Are comprehension skills practiced and maintained on a consistent basis through actual teaching activities?			
C. Do the guided reading comprehension questions relate to the main idea of a selection?			
D. Is there opportunity for students to apply comprehension skills in reading a total selection?			
E. Does the program provide help in the direct teaching of comprehension?			
F. Are comprehension questions clearly labeled?			
G. Are the skills that are labeled actually taught or merely mentioned?			
H. Is there opportunity to apply comprehension skills to outside reading?			
I. Are selections related to those read previously with questions that help children relate their ideas?			
J. Is there a clear relationship between vocabulary development and the comprehension instruction?			
K. Are writing and oral language activities used to reinforce comprehension?			

Criteria for Evaluating a Reading Program

	Series A	Series B	Series C
OTHER INSTRUCTIONAL CONSIDERATIONS			

Does the program provide for:

A. Clearly defined instruction? Is each important skill area adequately developed with:

   1. outcomes clearly stated?

   2. steps for teaching presented?

   3. provision for direct instruction?

   4. provision for related practice and application?

   5. provision for reteaching?

B. Language development?

   1. Is the interrelationship of oral language and reading stressed, particularly at early levels?

   2. Do children have opportunities to practice their reading vocabulary through use in oral and written language?

   3. Are writing and listening activities used to reinforce comprehension?

C. Practical application of basic reading skills?

   1. Are the study skills of locating and organizing information taught in the program?

   2. Is instruction provided in reading in content areas?

   3. Is attention directed to reading non-narrative, non-fiction, and content materials?

   4. Are varied and extensive activities provided for development of life and study skills?

   5. Are practical, real life contexts provided in which reading must be applied?

D. Literary understanding and appreciation?

   1. Is a variety of equality literature introduced throughout the program, including award-winning selections and classics for children?

   2. Do children learn to develop generalizations about literary forms and the author's craft?

   3. Does the program provide activities to develop literary understandings and appreciation?

   4. Does the program stimulate wide individual reading?

Criteria for Evaluating a Reading Program

	Series A	Series B	Series C

EVALUATION

Does the program provide these options?

A. An Informal Reading Inventory to assist teachers in assessing individual pupil behavior on materials which are to be used in learning to read?

B. A Placement Test to assist in placing pupils?

C. Specific evaluation and reinforcement activities at the end of units:

    1. in pupils' books?

    2. in Teachers' Editions?

    3. as test booklets?

    4. in other program materials?

D. Tests for each level of the program which measure growth from level to level (including growth in the critical reading skills)?

E. A recordkeeping instrument to chart learning progress?

F. A recordkeeping instrument to chart learning patterns?

G. Provision for feedback to pupils and teachers on pupil progress?

TEACHERS' EDITIONS

A. Is the Teacher's Edition

    1. easy to use?

    2. convenient to handle?

    3. clear in format?

    4. complete in providing needed help?

B. Does the Teacher's Edition combine readable reproductions of the pupil's pages with lesson plans?

C. Do they specify necessary as well as optional instructional procedures?

Criteria for Evaluating a Reading Program

	Series A	Series B	Series C
D. Are the Teacher's Editions practical? Do they include:			
1. an overview of the program?			
2. an overview of skills at the previous level?			
3. an overview of each level?			
4. an overview of each unit?			
5. an index to skills?			
6. cumulative vocabulary lists?			
7. specific instructional procedures for essential reading skill development?			
8. suggestions for reteaching, reinforcement, and enrichment activities?			
E. Does the Lesson Plan include:			
1. a list of new vocabulary?			
2. activities to develop skills in:			
a) decoding?			
b) vocabulary?			
c) comprehension?			
d) study skills and life skills?			
e) language development?			
f) literary understanding?			
TEACHING AIDS			
A. Are practice materials included to strengthen and enrich skill development and application?			
B. Are additional practice materials available to provide help in meeting individual needs?			
C. Are there Teachers' Editions of the Workbooks?			
D. Are there additional activities available in the Teachers' Editions to provide for individual student differences?			
E. Are supplementary materials carefully correlated with program instructions?			
F. Is there provision for parent involvement?			

Criteria for Evaluating a Reading Program

	Series A	Series B	Series C
VISUAL FEATURES			

A. Are the art and design colorful and attractive to children?

B. Do the illustrations support the content of the selections?

C. Does the visual design contribute to the teaching of the instructional program?

D. Do the illustrations show balanced variety in photographs, and art styles; in realistic and fanciful renderings; in physical, social, and geographical environments?

E. Is the type appropriately sized and spaced for the reading level?

F. Is the page arrangement constructed so that students can easily follow the flow?

Comments _____

_____

_____

_____

_____

_____

_____

_____

_____

_____

_____

_____

_____

_____

_____

_____

_____

_____

SINGLE OR MULTI-TEXT ADOPTIONS

Very often when the selection process is narrowed to two choices some people want to adopt both systems instead of one. If a multi-adoption is possible, then the programs should be different, not alike. If two programs remain "in the running," they are usually very much alike. Experience indicates that in such a case about half the people concerned would like to have both systems. This practice is *not* recommended.

The major disadvantage of multi-text adoption is that vocabulary words are not the same by level, especially at the first-grade level. In fact, Barnard and DeGracie (4) found that as many as two-thirds of the words are different. Also, the skills are not the same in different reading series, and this can cause reading retardation in the bottom third of a class.

The customary objection to a single adoption is that one series does not meet all the needs of all the students, but the truth is that it actually provides as well as another system would. True, one has to adjust instruction to meet needs, but a teacher would have to do that regardless of the textbooks used anyway. Almost all programs need supplements because they do not provide enough practice, especially for the bottom third of a class. It is easier and less costly to provide supplementary materials for one system than to purchase two entire systems.

A single adoption is also more efficient and effective than multi-adoptions in meeting student needs. And if students tend to move a great deal within a district, then a single adoption is even more logical. A multi-adoption is warranted only when the different programs are used in a strictly-tracked system. However, there is no need to track or buy more textbooks if teachers supplement the main text, especially for the bottom third, and assure mastery of vocabulary before proceeding.

Selecting Supplemental Materials

The money spent for basal materials is approximately the same per student in all districts. Great differences in per student cost are generally caused by supplemental material costs and amounts (8).

It is common for principals to hear pleas from teachers to buy materials they deem absolutely essential for success in the classroom. In some cases this may be true, but many times the materials will only add to the list of materials already on hand to teach a specific skill or concept. The degree of redundancy in our schools is tremendous.

It is not uncommon for a teacher to keep one set of materials and yet request another for the same purpose. For this reason alone you should continually evaluate supplementary material.

In general, teachers should be able to demonstrate the need for the materials they want. Have them evaluate two or three sets of material to fit this need rather than choose just one. Teachers should also check the evaluation file on supplements.

The following form can help people evaluate supplementary material. After evaluation, the form should be filed for others to refer to. In this way, you can avoid duplication in ordering supplementary material.

Figure 8-4: Evaluation of Supplemental Materials

(Rate on a 1-10 Scale)

FACTORS TO CONSIDER:	System A	System B	System C
1) Physical format. How will the material hold up?	_____	_____	_____
2) Where appropriate, is there a testing and student placement program?	_____	_____	_____
3) What is the interest level?	_____	_____	_____
4) What are the readability and vocabulary levels?	_____	_____	_____
5) Is there a skills program scope and sequence?	_____	_____	_____
6) Does it allow for individual progress?	_____	_____	_____
7) Are the illustrations appropriate?	_____	_____	_____
8) For what grade level(s) is the material best suited?	_____	_____	_____
9) Does the material allow for self-directing and self-correcting?	_____	_____	_____
10) Is it relevant for the local student population?	_____	_____	_____
11) Was the material field tested?	_____	_____	_____
12) Does this material fit the school philosophy and reading organization plan?	_____	_____	_____

13) Greatest strengths of the material:

System A _____

System B _____

System C _____

14) Greatest weaknesses of the material:

System A _____

System B _____

System C _____

15) Is there a need for this material? _____

16) Recommendation: _____

Managing Materials

The principal can avoid the proliferation of supplemental material by recording on a chart the basic program and supplementary materials used at each grade level. Such a chart, developed with the staff, also helps in avoiding conflict among teachers who believe others are using materials they should not be using. The following chart allows you to specify what materials are used (and in what sequence), and identify supplemental needs by grade level.

Once the chart is completed, it can guide those teachers using supplemental material along with specific parts of the basic program. In effect, the chart helps coordinate and match materials for maximum student benefit and avoids exposing students to the same material at different grade levels.

REFERENCES

1. Education, USA, Special Report, *Reading Crisis: The Problem and Suggested Solutions*. Washington, D.C.: National School Public Relations Association, 1970, p. 11.

2. Educational Products Information Exchange, *Protecting the Ultimate Educational Consumer—The Learner*. K. Komoski Testimony—House Select Committee on Education and Labor of the U. S. Congress. New York: Educational Products Information Exchange Institute, May, 1971, n. s.

3. Robert L. Hillerich, "So You're Evaluating Reading Programs!" *Elementary School Journal*, December, 1974, p. 1973.

4. Douglas P. Barnard and James S. DeGracie, "Vocabulary Analysis of New Primary Reading Series," *The Reading Teacher*, Vol. 30, (November, 1976), pp. 177–180.

5. George E. Mason, "Reading Series and Phonic Materials," Ph.D. dissertation, Syracuse University, 1963. *Dissertation Abstracts*, p. 5249.

6. Beatrict L. Kachuck, *Syntax Patterns in Elementary School Readers*, Final Report Project No. 4–0418, to U. S. Department of HEW, NIE. Brooklyn, N.Y., November 12, 1975, p. 8.

7. Robert A. Kaiser, Cheryl F. Neils, and Bernard P. Floriani, "Syntactic Complexity of Primary Grade Reading Materials: A Preliminary Look," *The Reading Teacher*, Vol. 29, (December, 1975), pp. 262–265.

8. Ernest Hilton, "Textbooks," in *Encyclopedia of Educational Research*, Ed. Robert L. Ebel. New York: Macmillan, 1969, p. 1473.

Figure 8–5: Sample Chart for Supplemental Materials Analysis

| BASIC PROGRAM | | | SUPPLEMENTAL MATERIALS | | | | | | |
| | | | SKILL BUILDING | | | | ENRICHMENT | |
Grade Level		Levels/Titles	Decoding	Comprehension	Vocabulary	Study Skills	Literature	Content Area
K	K	Animal Crackers						
1	1	One Potato Two						
	2	Little Dog Laughed						
	3	Fish and Not Fish						
	4	Inside My Hat						
	5	Birds Fly, Bears Don't						
	6	Across the Fence						
2	7	Glad to Meet You						
	8	Give Me a Clue						
3	9	Mystery Sneaker						
	10	Ten Times Round						
4	11	Barefoot Island						
5	12	Ride the Sunrise						
6	13	Flights of Color						
7	14	Green Salad Seasons						
8	15	Chains of Light						

9: Making Reading Visible and Viable

A major goal of reading instruction is to motivate children to read and to promote an interest in reading so that it becomes a lifelong habit. Although attitudes toward reading are greatly influenced by the home, the school can provide activities that stimulate interest and an on-going desire to read. To accomplish this, there is no better alternative than a teacher who is enthusiastic about reading and transmits this enthusiasm to children.

Artley (1) asked juniors and seniors majoring in a basic reading methods class what they could recall from their own experiences about how their teachers motivated them to read. The one activity that most of these majors remembered was their teachers' reading to the class. There is probably no easier way to kindle interest in reading than to read to a class. Teachers from all parts of the country recall this experience, more than any other, influencing their reading habits and attitudes. Teachers not only remember this special time in their lives, but also can recall the titles of the books read, even thirty or forty years afterwards. Clearly, the teacher's reading to the class should be an integral part of the daily reading program, if only for fifteen or twenty minutes each day.

Artley's students also mentioned the use of recognition, such as wall progress charts, certificates, gold stars, and graphs, as being motivational. Although this method worked for the brighter students, it was not so successful for others. Practices that provoked negative reactions from students were required book reports and reading aloud in front of the whole class (1).

Involving Parents and the Community

Because the influence of the home is so strong, the school should promote activities through which parents can support and encourage reading.

Many schools have developed excellent ideas to involve parents in their reading programs. The Reading Committee in Highland Park, Illinois proclaimed a Reading Awareness Week with the theme, "Have You Shared a Book Today?" (2). A letter was sent to parents explaining that each child would bring home a log for recording family reading activities during the week. There was a new activity for each day: Monday called for oral reading, Tuesday for periodicals, Wednesday for functional reading, Thursday for poetry, and Friday for reflection. At the end of the week, points were awarded to those who returned a completed log sheet, and this proved a powerful stimulus. Points were tallied by class, then for the whole school, and the total was recorded on a giant thermometer in the lobby of each school. This is just one example of the many kinds of activities that can involve parents in a school's reading program.

Some other examples might include:

READING FAIR

Newport News, Virginia coordinated its schools, parents, and community agencies, and invited local dignitaries to read to students for about thirty minutes at a local shopping mall. Children, teachers, and parents performed skits, and there were films of favorite children's stories. People dressed as book characters walked through the mall telling people about the fair. Local merchants gave discounts on books and provided giveaways such as bookmarks. This activity, conducted by Wilson-Gebhardt and Plowman (3), involved the community in making reading important for children.

BOOK EXCHANGE FAIR

Another successful activity is a school book fair. After collecting used paperback books from children and parents, set up the fair at a central location where children can buy or trade books. This is a popular approach and is yet another way to involve parents and the community in publicizing the importance of reading.

READING CONTRACTS

There are many variations of this endeavor that can involve parents or be just a school affair. Some schools send home a letter or contract asking parents to verify that the child has read for thirty minutes each night of the week. Asking parents to sign is an excellent method of showing parents that the school stresses reading. And if you wish to extend this idea, parents can contract with all family members to read for a given period. This could be parents' reading to their children, parents' listening to children read, or the whole family reading silently. Points and prizes can be awarded to sustain this activity for a longer period of time.

READ-A-THON

Read-A-Thons, often associated with certain medical foundations, do promote reading while at the same time earning money for the association. Some parents, however, object to their children's going door-to-door soliciting funds for a number of books to read. Misunderstanding can be avoided if a note is sent home asking parents to indicate whether they object to their child's being involved. This and other types of activities, whether fund-raising or not, create interest and motivation.

SCHOOL READ-IN

The school itself can designate a special area where four or five students may go to read during the school day. Students from various classrooms can read in this area from the beginning of the school to the end of the day, and even during the lunch hour and recess.

Reading Recognition—Awards and Ceremonies

Motivational devices, such as awarding reading certificates and prizes, do promote interest in reading, but may or may not involve parents in the community.

One enterprising reading teacher talked the parent-teachers organization into buying decals with the slogan "Read on Taft Tigers." These were then awarded for a certain number of books read, and star decals were offered for additional books. Parents reported that some children did not want the decal ironed on a T-shirt because it would wear off, so a certificate was also presented so that the students would have something to show for their efforts after the T-shirt was gone. Parents were intrigued and wanted to know if they, too, could earn a decal for reading a certain number of books, and some parents did indeed do just this!

This particular activity, designed by Marj Lott, a reading specialist in Mesa, Arizona, was extended to include writing skills. After a student read a book, he or she wrote and edited a synopsis and pasted it inside the front cover of the library book to guide others in their reading choices. The synopsis gave the main idea of the story and had to be legibly written, with correct punctuation, capitalization, and sentence structure.

A point to consider in any kind of reward structure is providing for *all* the students, so that those less able are not penalized for not achieving so well as the more able students. That is, some children might read 25 books for a prize, while others could earn it by reading five books.

If you use progress charts, they should be individual charts, and should not be posted in a room. Placing stars or other symbols next to a name can appear to be telling less able students that they are somehow not worthy, so the practice should be discouraged. Individual charts serve the same purpose and avoid the opportunity for comparisons by students and others, including parents.

Another successful activity is the holding of ceremonies at which awards or certificates are presented. One school planned a tea for parents in conjunction with its award ceremony. Teachers prepared refreshments and invited parents to come after school with their children. The principal then called up each child and gave the award for the number of books read. Surprisingly, parents took time off from work, packed the room every year for the ceremony, and beamed with pride as their child's name was read and the award presented.

SSR—Sustained Silent Reading

"SSR is a structured activity in which students are given a fixed period of time for silent reading of self-selected material" (4) (5). The concept is generally thought of as a 15–20-minute period of time during which all activities at a school cease and everyone, including the custodian, cafeteria workers, nurse, secretary, and principal, reads without interruption. The premise here is that too few students have role models outside of class, and that by seeing adults read at school their attitude toward, and interest in, reading will improve (6). Since the advent of SSR over a decade ago, many schools across the nation have made SSR a daily part of their reading program.

Junior Great Books Foundation

This non-profit foundation conducts workshops on interpretive and discussion techniques of classical literature for volunteers and teachers at all levels, grades two through twelve. The training is excellent and offers an added dimension to the reading program. Although some people see this as a program for gifted students, others consider it an integral part of the reading program for all students. Basically, it provides outstanding works of literature of the past that lend themselves to extended discussion. It teaches children to formulate and ask questions, as well as answer them, and it is excellent for the development of higher-level comprehension skills. More information is available from The Great Books Foundation, 307 North Michigan Avenue, Chicago, Illinois, 60601.

For reading to be *viable* for children, it must be *visible*. Children need to see that reading is more than just a school subject—that it is also a skill critical to learning and recreation. Today's society simply does not give children enough opportunities to see adults reading for either learning or enjoyment. The challenge is greater than simply teaching children to read; the challenge is teaching them to be readers.

REFERENCES

1. A. Sterl Artley, "Good Teachers of Reading—Who Are They?" *The Reading Teacher*, Vol. 29, No. 1, (October, 1975), pp. 26–31.

2. Mary Ann Manley and Alan E. Simon, "A Reading Celebration from K-8," *The Reading Teacher*, Vol. 33, No. 5, (February, 1980), pp. 552–554.

3. Concetta Wilson-Gebhardt and Corlea S. Plowman, "Tell Your Story with a Reading Fair," *The Reading Teacher*, Vol. 33, No. 5, (February, 1980), pp. 555–558.

4. Jesse C. Moore, Clarence J. Jones, and Douglas C. Miller, "What We Know After a Decade of Sustained Silent Reading," *The Reading Teacher*, Vol. 33, No. 4, (January, 1980), pp. 445–449.

5. Lyman C. Hunt, Jr., "The Effect of Self-Selection, Interest, and Motivation upon Independent, Instructional, and Frustrational Levels," *The Reading Teacher*, Vol. 24, No. 2, (November, 1970), pp. 146–151, 158.

6. Jesse C. Moore, Clarence J. Jones, and Douglas C. Miller, op. cit.

10: Fundamental Information for a Reading Professional— In Case I'm Asked, What Can I Say?

The field of reading instruction has been researched more than any other elementary school subject. Although the subject is complex, we will present the essence of it here, recognizing that certain concepts will be omitted that some might deem important. What takes place when a person reads has always been and continues to be a mystery. Scholars have attempted to bring coherence to the field by defining reading and the relationship among its major aspects, and by identifying the skills necessary to become an independent reader.

What Is Reading?

Clymer notes in his review of various reading models that, "There is no question more important to ask than: What is reading? Because of its implication for the instructional program, this question deserves and must have thoughtful attention" (1). Although models are useful devices in the study of a subject, for our purposes, we agree with Huus when she quotes Harris's definition of reading:

> The meaningful interpretation of written or printed verbal symbols. Reading involves sensing, perceiving, achieving, meaning, and reacting in a variety of ways. . . . Reading is accurate when the reader perceives the words as the author wrote them and the meaning he achieves corresponds closely to what the author intended. To this are added the reader's motor responses, his feelings, and his evaluation reactions (2).

Major Goals and Skills of Reading

The major goal of reading is to help every child read to the best of his or her ability. Achieving this and providing structure to the field embodies the concept of reading skills—the component skills of reading. The major reading skills are:

1. DECODING SKILLS — phonic and structural analysis of words

2. VOCABULARY DEVELOPMENT — sight and meaning of words

3. COMPREHENSION	literal, interpretive, experimental, and critical meanings of print
4. STUDY SKILLS	the tools and resources for academic learning (glossary, following directions, and so forth)
5. LIFE SKILLS	practical applications of reading skills (tax forms, bus schedules, and so on)
6. LITERATURE	appreciation of various literary forms
7. LANGUAGE ARTS	oral and written experience that involves the processing of ideas relating to reading

A more complete list of these reading skills, by levels, of the *Ginn Reading Program* and *Reading 720, Rainbow Edition* appears in Appendix B.

Definitions of Reading Terms

1. BACKGROUND EXPERIENCE	This is the composite of an individual's past distilled from the interaction with his or her environment, culture, language, thought patterns, and ideas on which new learnings build. The more varied the experiences, the greater the advantage for the child in relating to new experiences.
2. VISUAL DISCRIMINATION	This is the ability to *see* likenesses and differences in pictures, geometric shapes, letter forms, and word patterns.
3. AUDITORY DISCRIMINATION	This is the ability to *hear* likenesses and differences in sounds of all types, but particularly parts of words.
4. READINESS	This is the condition of being mature and motivated to learn new material without frustration.
5. BASAL READING PROGRAM	This is an instructional plan in which reading is taught through a series of graded readers. This developmental program teaches word identification and recognition, vocabulary, and comprehension skills, and fosters an interest in reading. About 85 percent of all students in the nation learn to read from a basal reading program.
6. PHONICS	This is the study of the sounds and spellings of word elements.
7. PHONETICS	This science of speech sounds deals with the way speech sounds are actually made. Training in phonetics is normally done by speech teachers.
8. PHONEME	This is the smallest unit of sound in spoken words.

9. VOWELS	Vowels are primarily sounds; they are represented by the vowel letters A, E, I, O, U, and sometimes W and Y.
10. LONG AND SHORT VOWEL SOUNDS	When sounding long vowels, one hears the name of the letter (in "mate," for example, the long "a" sound). The sound is of longer duration than that of a short vowel (in "mat," for example, the short "a" sound), which is spoken more quickly.
11. CONSONANTS	These are all letters other than vowels.
12. CONSONANT BLENDS	These are sounds of two or more letters that commonly occur together in a word; the identity of the letters is not lost (for example, cl-clear, tr-trap, sw-swim, spl-splash, and tw-twist).
13. R-CONTROLLED VOWEL	The English language contains many words in which a vowel sound is followed by an R sound that influences that sound in a special way, as in "car," "perk," "fir," "for," and "curl."
14. SCHWA SOUND (ə)	In many unaccented syllables, the vowel sound, regardless of the vowel letter, has a schwa sound that is a guttural, such as the first *a* in "*a*gain," "*a*bout," and in other words like "tul*i*p," "broad*e*n," and "cor*a*l."
15. DIGRAPHS	Two letters (vowels or consonants) that lose their individual identities and together stand for a single sound are digraphs. Examples are th, ch, sh, wh for consonants, and ea and oa, for vowels.
16. DIPHTHONGS	Two vowel sounds blending to make a gliding sound as *oy*, in "boy" and *ow* in "owl" are called diphthongs. Other diphthongs are *oi* and *ou*, as in "oie" and "you."
17. PHONOGRAM	Commonly called a word family, more accurately these are recognizable word elements that form a speech sound (*ack*-"back," *ill*-"till," "pill,").
18. SYLLABLE	A syllable may be a whole word or part of a word. It is a pronunciation unit composed of a vowel sound with or without one or more consonants.
19. ROOT	This is a base word from which other words, with changed meanings, can be made by adding prefixes and/or suffixes.
20. PREFIX	This is a letter, syllable, or group of syllables placed at the beginning of a root, changing the meaning (re-"regain," un-"unable").

21. SUFFIX

This is a letter, syllable, or group of syllables placed at the end of a root, changing the meaning (ness-"sickness," ful-"handful").

22. COMPOUND WORD

Two or more words that combine to make one word constitute a compound word ("air") and "port": "air-port").

23. STRUCTURAL ANALYSIS

This is the study of the structure of a word to note the root, prefix, suffix, inflected endings, and syllabication so that the word may be decoded.

24. SIGHT WORDS

These are the basic words that must be recognized as whole words on sight, without requiring decoding.

25. CONTEXT CLUES

These help identify the meaning of a word through its semantic or syntactic use in a sentence or longer context. Clues to word meaning are derived from the intent of the passage in which it appears.

26. LITERAL COMPREHENSION

This is the ability to recall specific information that is stated in a text, or to derive explicit meaning from material studied.

27. INFERENTIAL COMPREHENSION

This is the ability to infer meaning from information stated in a text, or to grasp solutions or outcomes implicit in material.

28. CRITICAL OR CREATIVE COMPREHENSION

The ability to formulate solutions based on a reader's own background of intelligence and experiences without reliance on outside material is called critical comprehension.

29. FOLLOW-UP

This is activity designed to strengthen abilities that have been introduced in a directed reading lesson, to provide needed practice, to broaden or deepen concepts, to provide additional experience, and to allow further related reading.

30. READING MANAGEMENT SYSTEM

This is a system of tests and record sheets designed to keep track of individual student skill needs as students progress through a reading program.

31. VAKT

This is a word learning technique that uses visual, auditory, kinesthetic, and tactile stimulation. The child learns by tracing words he pronounces himself, hears pronounced as they are written for him, and so on. Words come from his own oral language background and are learned and written to satisfy present needs. Specific training in this technique is required.

32. INFORMAL READING INVENTORY—IRI	This is a means of appraising reading levels, strengths, and weaknesses. A child reads graded selections of increasing difficulty. Through listening and interaction the examiner analyzes the child's current achievement in reading and determines his or her placement in a basal reader.
33. READABILITY LEVEL	This is an indication of the difficulty of reading material in terms of the grade level at which it is expected to be read. In most cases, the text is judged primarily by the difficulty of its vocabulary and the length and complexity of its sentences.
34. INDEPENDENT READING LEVEL	This is the reading level at which a child can function comfortably with no teacher help. Word recognition should be 99% accurate; comprehension of all types should average at least 90%.
35. INSTRUCTIONAL READING LEVEL	This is the reading level at which a child can function adequately with teacher guidance and, at the same time, meet enough challenges to stimulate further growth. On a pretest at this level, word recognition should be 95% accurate and comprehension at least 75%.
36. FRUSTRATION LEVEL	This is the reading level at which the child's ability to read disintegrates. Word recognition falls to 90% or below, and comprehension to 50% or below. Many other symptoms (some severe) such as problems in vocalization, tension movements, and so forth may appear.

Answers to Some Common Questions

Over the years, we have been asked many questions, some of which we have tried to answer in earlier chapters. The intent of this chapter is to address certain other questions frequently asked and not treated elsewhere in the book. The responses, it should be stated, are *not* exhaustive; rather, the intention here is to provide a succinct comment that captures the essence of the issue.

1. IS THERE ONE BEST WAY TO TEACH READING?

It is often said that there is no single best way to teach beginning reading — that it is the teacher who is more important than the approach. This is trite, but true.

All of the various methods of teaching reading can be classified as either *synthetic* or *analytical*.

SYNTHETIC	A phonic, code-emphasis approach in which children learn the sounds of letters that are blended into words. The primary emphasis is on decoding words and then teaching comprehension.
ANALYTICAL	A look-say, meaning-emphasis approach in which children learn a few sight words that are later analyzed into phonemic elements. The primary emphasis is on meaning first, then on phonic analysis.

103

Both approaches teach phonics and comprehension. The difference lies in what they emphasize initially.

The Cooperative Research Program in First Grade Reading Instruction, involving over 20,000 students and 27 separate research projects, concluded that the phonics-related approaches generally developed superior word recognition skills compared to the basal programs. The study concluded, however, that, "No one approach is so distinctly better in all situations and respects than the others that it should be considered the one best method and the one to be used exclusively" (3). In fact, Bond and Dykstra conclude that:

> Combinations of programs, such as a basal program with supplementary phonics material, often are superior to single approaches. Furthermore, the success of such methods as the Language Experience approach indicates that the addition of language experience to any kind of reading program can be expected to make a contribution (4).

Contemporary basal reading programs have tended to include more phonics earlier than in the past, and phonics-method programs have included more meaning or comprehension activity. Both approaches are effective, and we appear to have as many poor and good readers with one approach as with the other. We have to agree with Chall, Bond, and Dykstra that it is the *overall* competence of the teacher that makes the difference (5). As Margaret Early emphasized, "If research says anything to teachers, it is don't go overboard. In reading, keep an eye on decoding and meaning" (6).

2. SHOULD LETTER NAMES OR LETTER SOUNDS BE TAUGHT IN KINDERGARTEN?

The teaching of letter names *should* precede the teaching of letter sounds because the former are more stable. Each letter has only one name regardless of its location, whereas some letters require more than one single sound. There is much research supporting the teaching of letter names and the correlation of this skill to later reading achievement (7) (8) (9). Bond and Dykstra note that, "The knowledge of letter names gained prior to initial instruction alone would account for approximately 25 to 36 percent of the variation in reading ability found at the end of the [first] year . . ." (10). Weaver and Shonkoff also stress the importance of letter names: "Most important, the letter names should be taught during kindergarten because letter name knowledge is necessary for communication between the teacher and the student during reading and language instruction" (11).

The debate may be academic, because many children enter kindergarten already knowing many letters of the alphabet. Once the names of the letters are mastered, it is easy to move on to teaching individual letter sounds and blending.

3. OF WHAT VALUE ARE READING GAMES?

The primary value of games is to stimulate interest and provide practice in reading skills. Unfortunately, some teachers use games before a child has a firm grasp of the concept. Games can be misused and should be reserved mostly for the practice of individual skills.

4. WHY DO ACHIEVEMENT SCORES DECLINE IN THE INTERMEDIATE GRADES?

We must recognize that the difficulty of materials increases markedly from grade three to grade four. In grade four, print is usually smaller, there is more of it on the page, and the maturity level of the text is more advanced. Therefore, students who were marginal at third grade do not perform so well as other students when encountering this abrupt jump in reading difficulty.

A second factor is the assumption that the previous emphasis on learning to read should change to reading to learn. Thus there is less emphasis on teaching and more emphasis on covering content. Students become more involved with filling in blanks. It is common for intermediate teachers to talk about skills or concepts, but then engage the students in a practice or assessing activity without giving enough direct instruction (12). Missing in too many intermediate classrooms is the full process of teaching, explaining, modeling, asking probing questions, and giving students feedback—all of which is just as critical at the intermediate grades as at the primary levels. It is this lack of instructional interaction that probably causes not only the decline in achievement, but also the decline of students' interest in school. Students need to be *involved* and need to be *instructed* if achievement is to be a reality.

5. HOW CRITICAL ARE BEHAVIORAL OBJECTIVES, AND DOES THIS LISTING OF SKILLS FRAG-MENT READING INSTRUCTION?

The listing of instructional objectives is critical and essential for any instructional program. The listing of such skills in *behavioral* terms, however, has little value except for test makers. Very few teachers use behavioral objectives, but most teachers do use instructional objectives—the skills or concepts they wish to teach.

Indeed, the listing and testing of reading subskills can lead to teaching subskills in isolation from reading as a whole. Teaching reading subskills is essential, but the problem arises when these skills are not practiced and integrated with the act of reading. Weaver and Shonkoff emphasize that, "The important thing to remember is that although reading may be taught subskill by subskill, students should always have ample opportunity to practice the whole activity" (13).

6. OF WHAT VALUE ARE MACHINES?

Machines are like games—if used to motivate and provide practice and reinforcement, they have a place in the reading program. Overuse or misuse of machines wastes resources, but with proper use they are stimulating and can free the teachers for directed instruction with other students.

7. HOW CAN THE SIZE OF READING GROUPS BE REDUCED TO MAKE INSTRUCTION EASIER FOR THE TEACHER?

In essence, the question is "How can one find more instructional time?" Short of adding hours to the school day, there are realistic means available within the school organization to do this.

1. There can be staggered starting times, even for those on bus schedules, so that the teacher has fewer children at the beginning and end of the day.

2. The scheduling of the physical education, music, art, and other special courses can be adjusted so that teachers can have fewer students to work with at a time. For instance, instead of sending an entire class for a special activity, arrange to have half, a third, or some other number with the teacher.

3. Use parent volunteers to take a certain group for an activity, so the teacher can work with the remaining group.

There are various ways to reduce the number of students teachers work with at one time, but it does require organization and the cooperation of teachers with one another.

8. SHOULD TEACHERS COVER THE ENTIRE BOOK AT A GIVEN GRADE LEVEL?

Yes and no. If student needs are being met, as discussed in Chapter Five, some students will cover more than the grade-level materials and other students will not finish even one-half of the material.

9. A READING MANAGEMENT SYSTEM HAS HUNDREDS OF OBJECTIVES, AND THE TEACHERS IGNORE THE SYSTEM. IS THE MANAGEMENT SYSTEM NECESSARY?

Yes, there *must* be a management system in order to realize fully both instruction and achievement. Whether this system is minimal or highly-segmented is another question. Reading management systems with over 25 objectives per level are very seldom successful. Tracking students with 25 or fewer major objectives, however, is manageable and can be successful. Tracking students with too many objectives and tests results in teachers' rejecting or sabotaging the system.

10. HOW IMPORTANT IS READABILITY?

Knowing the readability level helps match the reading level of students with the reading level of the material (14). Although this is the goal of readability, there are a host of factors that should be considered, because readability formulae usually do not involve much more than sentence length and the number of syllables in words. "High motivation overcomes high readability, but low motivation demands a low readability level" (15). Russell and Fea, in investigating several readability formulae, state that these formulae do not:

1. Give any measure of conceptual difficulty in textbook material.

2. Take into consideration the way the material is organized or arranged.

3. Allow for variations in the meaning of words with multiple meanings.

4. Accept the fact that a fresh or unusual word may make a sentence or idea clearer than a commonplace word.

5. Vary their ratings in terms of different interests that persons may have at different developmental levels nor in terms of individual activities.

6. Take account of physical factors such as format and illustrations (16).

Since the popular readability formulae used today do not consider many variables, readability should be regarded as a rough indication of reading level, not as an absolute.

11. WHAT PLACE DOES ORAL READING HAVE IN THE READING PROGRAM?

Oral reading is a valuable reading skill and should be part of the reading program, especially at the primary-grade levels. At these levels, oral reading is practiced daily, because children read aloud in their reading groups. The major goal at this level is to check and diagnose word recognition skills. As students progress through the grades, oral reading decreases and silent reading becomes more dominant. About four-fifths of the reading instructional time is spent on oral reading at the primary level and about one-fifth at the intermediate levels.

There are, however, some oral reading practices that tend to have a *negative* effect on children, especially on the less able. The major culprit here is round robin reading, in which each child in the class takes turns reading while the others follow along (17). This should *not* be an activity for the whole class. Less able students should practice oral reading in smaller instructional groups or individually in order for the teacher to check decoding needs.

Ammon claims there are essentially three reasons for oral reading: "To entertain, to share information, and for the teacher to help the child with reading" (18).

The skills of oral reading (proper eye span, phrasing, looking up, and expression) are valuable skills, especially for the average and above-average students who are most likely to need such skills in the future. As a courtesy, students should also have the opportunity to preread a selection before reading orally to a group, unless this is a test.

12. ARE "MASTERY LEARNING" AND "COMPETENCY TESTING" THE SAME THING?

Although a student must demonstrate competency or mastery of a skill before proceeding to the next skill level, the terms are not synonymous. Mastery learning is based on the assumption that given enough time and appropriate instruction, nearly all students can learn. Mastery learning is an instructional system composed of objectives, diagnoses, prescription, assessment, feedback, and recordkeeping and reporting systems. These components ensure that every student is working at his or her instructional level and continues until the assessment shows that the student has mastered a given skill. In essence, mastery learning is just good teaching in which a student's progress is judged individually, not against a norm on a test.

Competency testing is merely assessment of a competency, usually a minimum competency. In this sense, it can be considered the assessment part of a mastery learning plan. Competency testing is *not* an instructional *system*, but only *one* of the components within it. It will identify problems, but it is not usually diagnostic, nor does it meet individual needs. Competency testing tells us when a student has or does not have a given competency.

We should also mention that competency testing serves an accountability function that increasingly larger numbers of legislators across the country seem to feel is necessary. It is the public that wants to determine how well students are performing against some standard, and thus it has limited value from an educational point of view. Mastery learning, on the other hand, is a teaching strategy that has the potential to significantly improve educational services for children.

REFERENCES

1. Theodore W. Clymer, "What Is Reading?: Some Current Concepts," *Innovation and Change in Reading Instruction*, the Sixty-Seventh Yearbook of the National Society for the Study of Education, Part II. Chicago: The University of Chicago Press, 1968, p. 29.

2. Albert J. Harris, *Effective Teaching of Reading*. New York: David McKay, 1962, p. 13, cited by Helen Huus, "Basic Reading Skill Instruction in the Total Curriculum," *Reading and the Elementary School Curriculum*, Ed. David L. Sheperd. Newark, Delaware: International Reading Association, 1969, p. 26.

3. Guy L. Bond and Robert Dykstra, "The Cooperative Research Program in First Grade Reading Instruction," *Reading Research Quarterly*, Vol. 2, No. 4, (Summer, 1967), p. 123.

4. Ibid., p. 122.

5. Education, USA, *Reading Crisis: The Problem and Suggested Solutions*. Washington, D.C.: National School Public Relations Association, 1970, pp. 46–47.

6. Margaret Early, "Important Research in Reading and Writing," *Phi Delta Kappan*, Vol. 57, No. 5, (January, 1976), p. 301.

7. Ralph A. Dermott, "Two Dimensions of Field Dependence-Independence: How They and Nine Other Variables Interrelate and Predict Specific Reading Skills at the End of the First Grade." Ed.D. dissertation, University of Maine, 1977.

8. Sigmar Muehl and Mario C. DiNello, "Early First Grade Skills Related to Subsequent Reading Performance: A Seven-Year Follow-Up Study," *Journal of Reading Behavior*, (Spring, 1976), pp. 67–81.

9. Thomas L. Hick and Marilyn C. Stantman, "Test of a Strategy to Increase the Predictability of First Grade Reading Skills from Letter Naming Abilities to Kindergarten," *The Journal of Educational Research*, Vol. 65, No. 4, (December, 1971), pp. 147–150.

10. Guy L. Bond and Robert Dykstra, op. cit., p. 117.

11. Phyllis Weaver and Fredi Shonkoff, *Research Within Reach—A Research-Guided Response to Concerns of Reading Educators*. St. Louis, Mo.: CEMREL, Inc., and National Institute of Education, 1978, p. 37.

12. Dolores Durkin, "What Classroom Observations Reveal About Reading Comprehension Instruction," *Reading Research Quarterly*, Vol. 14, No. 4, (1978–79), pp. 481–533.

13. Phyllis Weaver and Frede Shonkoff, op. cit., p. 7.

14. Edward Fry, "The Readability Principle," *Language Arts*, Vol. 52, (September, 1975), pp. 847–851.

15. Ibid.

16. Roger Farr, *Reading: What Can Be Measured*. Newark, Delaware: International Reading Association, 1970, p. 18.

17. A. Sterl Artley, "Good Teachers of Reading—Who Are They?" *The Reading Teacher*, Vol. 29, No. 1, (October, 1975), pp. 26–31.

18. Richard Ammon, "Queries—Why Oral Reading," *Language Arts*, Vol. 56, No. 8, (November/December, 1979), p. 952.

Appendix A: Goals and Objectives of the *Ginn Reading Program*

Ginn and Company believes that a basal reading program should have six essential characteristics:

1. Active content, including selections and illustrations by award-winning authors and illustrators, to engage children in a rich variety of fiction and non-narrative reading experiences.

2. A blending of high-utility skills, taught in meaningful contexts, to lead children to early independence in reading.

3. Comprehension strategies, to stimulate children's thinking and reasoning skills.

4. Assessment tools that give teachers and administrators effective ways to manage instruction.

5. Approaches and materials to meet individual needs, including those of the below-average child and the gifted and talented.

6. Tools for teaching that provide teachers with concise suggestions and clearly-focused lesson plans.

In designing the *Ginn Reading Program* to accomplish these goals, Ginn and Company relied especially on the following research-based findings.

Research-Based Decisions

COMPREHENSION

- A pupil's prior knowledge affects his or her comprehension. One goal of a total reading program must be to build the necessary knowledge base; another to develop in children purposes for reading particular selections so as to help them relate what they read to their prior knowledge.

- The purpose that a reader brings to reading a text strongly affects his or her comprehension of the text.

- Children must be taught strategies of comprehension that apply to words, statements, and longer selections.

- Most comprehension involves some degree of inferential thinking, of grasping meanings that lie under the surface of a statement. Literal comprehension and inferential comprehension thus exist largely on a continuum stretching from directly-stated literal meaning through increasingly complex implied meanings.

- The ability to comprehend involves more than mastery of a diverse set of specific skills. Children must learn how to integrate many specific skills in understanding a single selection. Effective comprehension involves interaction between general schema-driven processes and text-driven processes.

- Organization of reading selections into topical or thematic units can help children relate ideas in one selection to those encountered in others and thus support relating reading to prior experience.

- Children's expectations concerning the organization of stories (story grammars) affect their comprehension of stories. By directing the children's attention to certain nearly universal story features, teachers can build sets of useful expectations.

- Questioning can influence comprehension. The kinds of questions that teachers ask will influence how children learn.

- By using a carefully-selected series of questions to build a "story map," or recreation of the important elements of the text, teachers can help pupils apply a variety of sub-skills in the context of total comprehension.

- Children need direct instruction and practice in comprehending non-narrative as well as narrative selections. Skills needed in comprehension vary with different modes of discourse or varieties of text structure.

- Language learning is closely associated with learning to think. It is important, therefore, to stress continually the importance of thinking and reasoning while reading.

- Writing about what one reads can support the comprehension process. Writing that involves summarizing or the reprocessing of ideas is especially effective.

- Children's comprehension increases to the extent that they are asked to perform inferential elaborations and manipulations while reading.

DECODING

- An early systematic emphasis on decoding is essential in teaching beginning reading.

- Phonics instruction and reading for meaning are interdependent and mutually supportive instructionally. From the beginning children must learn to decode with meaning.

- Those basic skills that are known to be necessary for successful reading must and can be taught directly at the kindergarten level, or before children begin formal reading instruction.

- Children need direct instruction in auditory segmentation, letter and sound mapping, and strategies for decoding polysyllables.

- Instructional focus should be placed on the high-utility skills.

- Practice in writing theoretically decodeable words in sentences provides opportunities for children to apply reading and writing skills in meaningful contexts.

VOCABULARY

- A lexicon required for today's reading instruction not only must be based on extant word lists, but also on the words children have added to their speaking and listening vocabularies as a result of years of television viewing.

- Direct instruction in comprehension of vocabulary is essential and provides a way of integrating many of the distinct processes involved in reading.

- Performance surveys have identified those words mastered by the great majority of first graders, second graders, and third graders. These can be used as one basis of the vocabulary in a basal reading program.

- More attention needs to be paid to the multiple meanings of words. Of the 3000 or so words that are most frequently used, approximately 25% are multiple-meaning words.

- Instruction in critical vocabulary must be given before pupils read a selection, with attention to using diverse methods of unlocking the meanings of the words.

- Planned maintenance of basic vocabulary occurs only as children keep meeting the words they have learned.

- Because prior knowledge of vocabulary (particularly idiomatic expressions) relates in part to a child's prior social and economic experience, teachers should be alert to the need to cope with the varieties of language experience among children with various backgrounds.

- Children effectively learn the meanings of vocabulary by using the terms in processing language in writing. This is an especially effective way of acquiring technical vocabulary.

INSTRUCTION

- Direct instruction by the teacher is mandatory in improving student learning.

- A limited number of high-priority skills outcomes must be identified for instruction. Effective instruction requires focusing on essential skills, not "exposure" to many.

- Instruction, practice, and application activities in teaching reading must be focused on those skills and attitudes that we want children to learn.

- Effective reading practice is practice that immediately follows and relates to direct instruction. Such practice needs to be sufficiently massed within a short period of time so that most children can master the target skill.

- The amount of practice children need in reading will vary with their success in learning to read. Poor readers will require much more practice than will good readers.

- The flow of instruction—its organization, the directions required by teachers and pupils—needs to be field-tested to verify its effectiveness.

- Noninstructional time and noninstructional activities must be reduced if teaching effectiveness is to improve.

- Systematic and formal methods for teaching beginning reading are more effective for most children than are informal approaches.

- Children need to understand which skills they are expected to master and to receive feedback on their progress approximately every two weeks.

- Most children profit from an abundance of easy practice. At the primary level, about two-thirds of the practice should be easy.

- Instruction in needed skills should occur before reading so that children can use the skills during reading. This is especially important in acquiring new vocabulary and in developing decoding skills.

- Children must not only practice basic reading skills in academic contexts, but must also learn to apply these skills to life. Effective reading programs must teach applications of skills.

- Because children spend approximately a third of their time completing workbooks and activity sheets, much more care needs to be taken to ensure that these instructional materials provide significant practice of skills.

- Instructional materials must be designed to permit flexible use by the classroom teacher.

LIFE AND STUDY SKILLS

- Studies of the literacy skills required in life help to identify important skills to be taught and assessed in a reading program.

- Life skills and study skills should be taught as applications of basic reading skills.

- Life skills are most effectively taught when information is presented in well-understood contexts.

- Children need to learn how to learn by developing the strategies of predicting, checking, planning, and monitoring their own knowledge as they read.

ASSESSMENT

- Mastery learning in reading requires outcome-oriented instruction on selected, high-priority skills; related drill, practice and application of the target skills; criterion-referenced testing to ascertain each pupil's degree of mastery; and provision for second instruction and variable practice, according to the needs of each learner.

- The basic skills selected for emphasis are those essential to reading and assessed in most survey tests and state assessment tests.

- Teachers should *not* receive detailed data concerning pupils' progress more frequently than they are prepared to make instructional decisions on the basis of it.

- To teach diagnostically, teachers need appropriate tools and detailed recommendations.

LITERATURE

- A child's ability to enter into the literary experience will depend in large measure on the points of contact between the text and the child's own experience.

- Familiarity with the best-known folk tales, myths, and legends—reservoir literature—provides needed background for understanding the many allusions to such literature in adult reading.

- It is the literary work itself and the child's experience with the work that must be the focus of instruction.

- Overemphasis on facts about a literary work, on background details, on authors, and on literary form can distract readers from the experience of literature.

- Children are more likely to learn to read if asked to read selections that relate to their interests and experiences.

- Tryout of proposed reading selections with children at various age levels helps determine which selections teachers and pupils like best, as well as which ones need special instructional approaches.

RELATED LANGUAGE ARTS

- Listening comprehension and reading comprehension are closely related. Direct teaching of listening comprehension thus results in improved reading comprehension.

- Writing that involves the reprocessing of ideas from reading supports reading comprehension. Most children have too few opportunities to reprocess their ideas in writing.

- Encouraging children to elaborate on their reading during discussion can lead to improvements in their comprehension.

- Oral reading by the teacher and interpretive reading by children can help in developing sensitivity to the creative uses of language.

Appendix B: List of Ginn Reading Materials

The Ginn Reading Program 1982©

Placement Materials

Placement Test (pkg. of 25 booklets, manual, key)	39482-1
Placement Test (Spirit Duplication Masters) and 2 Manuals with Key	39488-0
Manual and Key for Placement Test (pkg. of 5)	39493-7
Informal Reading Inventory for Levels 3-13	39480-5

Parent/Home Package

Parent/Home Activity Sheets

Kindergarten (16 pads, 24 sheets per pad)	39575-5
Grade 1 (20 pads, 24 sheets per pad)	39582-8
Grade 2 (16 pads, 24 sheets per pad)	39587-9
Grade 3 (16 pads, 24 sheets per pad)	39592-5
Grade 4 (16 pads, 24 sheets per pad)	39598-4
Grade 5 (16 pads, 24 sheets per pad)	39604-2
Grade 6 (16 pads, 24 sheets per pad)	39609-3

Parent/Home Newspapers

Kindergarten (3 issues, pkgs. of 24 each)	39615-8
Grade 1 (3 issues, pkgs. of 24 each)	39620-4
Grade 2 (3 issues, pkgs. of 24 each)	39625-5
Grade 3 (3 issues, pkgs. of 24 each)	39632-8
Grade 4 (3 issues, pkgs. of 24 each)	39637-9
Grade 5 (3 issues, pkgs. of 24 each)	39642-5
Grade 6 (3 issues, pkgs. of 24 each)	39648-4

Kindergarten
ANIMAL CRACKERS KINDERGARTEN KIT

Complete Kit: Teacher's Edition, Story/Language Posters, Display Board, Record, Story Characters, Game Boards, Alphabet Cards, Story/Language Cards, Picture-Word Cards, Letters, Numbers, Shapes, Concept Cards, Worksheets (56 pads, 25 sheets per pad)	38123-1

Animal Crackers Kit components available separately

Teacher's Edition	38054-5
Story/Language Posters (pkg. of 20 illustrations on 10 posters)	38094-4
Alphabet Cards (pkg. of 26 cards)	38066-9
Story/Language Cards (pkg. of 20 illustrations on 10 cards)	38071-5
Picture-Word Cards (pkg. of 36 cards)	38082-0
Letters (2 sets each capital and lower case letters)	38077-4
Numbers (2 sets of 10 cards)	38121-5
Shapes (pkg. of 24 cards)	38104-5

Kindergarten Parent/Home Activity Sheets (16 pads, 24 sheets per pad)	39575-5
Kindergarten Parent/Home Newspaper (3 issues, pkgs. of 24 each)	39615-8

Level 1

ONE POTATO, TWO

Write-in Text (consumable)	38160-6
Teacher's Edition	38165-7
Level 1 Test (pkg. of 25 booklets, manual, key)	38174-6
Manual with Key for Level 1 Test (separate)	38177-0
Big Book	39818-5
Worksheets Spirit Duplication Masters (boxed set of 76)	38182-7
Reading Progress Cards (pkg. of 100) for Levels 1-15	39499-6
Individual Skills Inventory Cards (pkg. of 100) for Levels 1-13	39501-1
Card Set (Pictures, Words, Punctuation)	38188-6
Grade 1 Parent/Home Activity Sheets (20 pads, 24 sheets per pad)	39582-8
Grade 1 Parent/Home Newspaper (3 issues, pkgs. of 24 each)	39620-4

Level 2

LITTLE DOG LAUGHED

(paperbound)	38193-2
Teacher's Edition	38198-3
*Skillpack Booklet	38203-3
Teacher's Edition of Skillpack Booklet	38214-9
Skillpack Spirit Duplication Masters (boxed set of 44)	38209-2
Studybook (Workbook)	38226-2
Teacher's Edition of Studybook	38231-9
Big Book	39823-1
Level 2 Test (pkg. of 25 booklets, manual, key)	38265-3
Manual with Key for Level 2 Test (separate)	38269-6
Unit Tests (12 Test booklets, 1 Class Record Sheet, 1 Unit Test Manual and Key)	
Concept Cards (set of 4 decks)	38087-1
Worksheets (56 pads, 25 sheets per pad)	38099-5

Animal Crackers

Write-in Text (consumable)	38127-4
Teacher's Edition	38132-0
Kindergarten Test (pkg. of 25 booklets, manual, key)	38140-1
Manual with Key for Kindergarten Test (separate)	38144-4
Form A	38239-4
Form B	38244-0

Appears in Teacher's Edition of text

Code Number

The Ginn Reading Program Continued

Booster Activities (1 pkg. of 24 Spirit
Duplication Masters and Manual).... 38220-3

Reading Progress Cards
(pkg. of 100) for Levels 1-15 39499-6

Individual Skills Inventory Cards
(pkg. of 100) for Levels 1-13 39501-1

Pupil Profile Card (pkg. of 100)
for Levels 2-15 39496-1

Instructional Wall Charts 39751-0

Grade 1 Parent/Home Activity
Sheets (20 pads, 24 sheets per pad) 39582-8

Grade 1 Parent/Home Newspaper
(3 issues, pkgs. of 24 each) 39620-4

Card Set Levels 2-4 39505-4

Level 3

FISH AND NOT FISH
(paperbound) 38280-7

Teacher's Edition 38286-6

*Skillpack Booklet 38291-2

Teacher's Edition of Skillpack
Booklet 38302-1

Skillpack Spirit Duplication Masters
(boxed set of 60) 38296-3

Studybook (Workbook) 38313-7

Teacher's Edition of Studybook 38319-6

Level 3 Test (pkg. of 25 booklets,
manual, key) 38355-2

Manual with Key for Level 3 Test
(separate) 38358-7

Unit Tests (12 Test booklets, 1 Class
Record Sheet, 1 Unit Test Manual
and Key)
Form A 38327-7
Form B.......... 38332-3

Booster Activities (1 pkg. of 32 Spirit
Duplication Masters and Manual).... 38308-0

Reading Progress Cards
(pkg. of 100) for Levels 1-15 39499-6

Individual Skills Inventory Cards
(pkg. of 100) for Levels 1-13 39501-1

Pupil Profile Card (pkg. of 100) for
Levels 2-15 39496-1

Instructional Wall Charts.............. 39756-1

Informal Reading Inventory for
Levels 3-13 39480-5

Grade 1 Parent/Home Activity
Sheets (20 pads, 24 sheets per pad) 39582-8

Grade 1 Parent/Home Newspaper
(3 issues, pkgs. of 24 each) 39620-4

Card Set Levels 2-4 39505-4

Level 4

INSIDE MY HAT (paperbound) 38369-2

Teacher's Edition 38374-9

*Skillpack Booklet 38380-3

Teacher's Edition of Skillpack
Booklet 38391-9

Skillpack Spirit Duplication Masters
(boxed set of 60) 38386-2

Studybook (Workbook) 38403-6

Teacher's Edition of Studybook 38408-7

Level 4 Test (pkg. of 25 booklets,
manual, key) 38443-5

Manual with Key for Level 4 Test
(separate) 38447-8

Code Number

Unit Tests (12 Test booklets, 1 Class
Record Sheet, 1 Unit Test Manual
and Key)
Form A 38416-8
Form B.......... 38421-4

Booster Activities (1 pkg. of 32 Spirit
Duplication Masters and Manual).... 38397-8

Reading Progress Cards
(pkg. of 100) for Levels 1-15 39499-6

Individual Skills Inventory Cards
(pkg. of 100) for Levels 1-13 39501-1

Pupil Profile Card (pkg. of 100)
for Levels 2-15 39496-1

Instructional Wall Charts 39763-4

Informal Reading Inventory for
Levels 3-13 39480-5

Grade 1 Parent/Home Activity
Sheets (20 pads, 24 sheets per pad) 39582-8

Grade 1 Parent/Home Newspaper
(3 issues, pkgs. of 24 each) 39620-4

Card Set Levels 2-4 39505-4

Level 5

BIRDS FLY, BEARS DON'T
(hardbound) 38457-5

Teacher's Edition 38462-1

*Skillpack Booklet 38468-0

Teacher's Edition of Skillpack
Booklet 38479-6

Skillpack Spirit Duplication Masters
(boxed set of 108) 38473-7

Studybook (Workbook) 38490-7

Teacher's Edition of Studybook 38496-6

Level 5 Test (pkg. of 25 booklets,
manual, key) 38531-8

Manual with Key for Level 5 Test
(separate) 38534-2

Unit Tests (12 Test booklets, 1 Class
Record Sheet, 1 Unit Test Manual
and Key)
Form A 38503-2
Form B.......... 38508-3

Booster Activities (1 pkg. of 48 Spirit
Duplication Masters and Manual).... 38485-0

Reading Progress Cards
(pkg. of 100) for Levels 1-15 39499-6

Individual Skills Inventory Cards
(pkg. of 100) for Levels 1-13 39501-1

Pupil Profile Card (pkg. of 100)
for Levels 2-15 39496-1

Instructional Wall Charts 39768-5

Informal Reading Inventory for
Levels 3-13 39480-5

Grade 1 Parent/Home Activity
Sheets (20 pads, 24 sheets per pad) 39582-8

Grade 1 Parent/Home Newspaper
(3 issues, pkgs. of 24 each) 39620-4

Card Set Levels 5 and 6 39510-0

Level 6

ACROSS THE FENCE (hardbound) 38545-8

Teacher's Edition 38550-4

*Skillpack Booklet 38555-5

Teacher's Edition of Skillpack
Booklet 38567-9

Skillpack Spirit Duplication Masters
(boxed set of 124) 38562-8

Studybook (Workbook) 38578-4

*Appears in Teacher's Edition of text

The Ginn Reading Program Continued

Teacher's Edition of Studybook	38583-0
Level 6 Test (pkg. of 25 booklets, manual, key)	38619-5
Manual with Key for Level 6 Test (separate)	38622-5
Unit Tests (12 Test booklets, 1 Class Record Sheet, 1 Unit Test Manual and Key)	
Form A	38591-1
Form B	38597-0
Booster Activities (1 pkg. of 46 Spirit Duplication Masters and Manual)	38572-5
Reading Progress Cards (pkg. of 100) for Levels 1-15	39499-6
Individual Skills Inventory Cards (pkg. of 100) for Levels 1-13	39501-1
Pupil Profile Card (pkg. of 100) for Levels 2-15	39496-1
Instructional Wall Charts	39773-1
Informal Reading Inventory for Levels 3-13	39480-5
Grade 1 Parent/Home Activity Sheets (20 pads, 24 sheets per pad)	39582-8
Grade 1 Parent/Home Newspaper (3 issues, pkgs. of 24 each)	39620-4
Card Set Levels 5 and 6	39510-0

Level 7

GLAD TO MEET YOU (hardbound)	38633-0
Teacher's Edition	38638-1
*Skillpack Booklet	38645-4
Teacher's Edition of Skillpack Booklet	38655-1
Skillpack Spirit Duplication Masters (boxed set of 140)	38650-0
Studybook (Workbook)	38666-7
Teacher's Edition of Studybook	38671-3
Level 7 Test (pkg. of 25 booklets, manual, key)	38707-8
Manual with Key for Level 7 Test (separate)	38710-8
Unit Tests (12 Test booklets, 1 Class Record Sheet, 1 Unit Test Manual and Key)	
Form A	38679-9
Form B	38684-5
Booster Activities (1 pkg. of 45 Spirit Duplication Masters and Manual)	38661-6
Reading Progess Cards (pkg. of 100) for Levels 1-15	39499-6
Individual Skills Inventory Cards (pkg. of 100) for Levels 1-13	39501-1
Pupil Profile Card (pkg. of 100) for Levels 2-15	39496-1
Instructional Wall Charts	39779-0
Informal Reading Inventory for Levels 3-13	39480-5
Grade 2 Parent/Home Activity Sheets (16 pads, 24 sheets per pad)	39587-9
Grade 2 Parent/Home Newspaper (3 issues, pkgs. of 24 each)	39625-5

Level 8

GIVE ME A CLUE (hardbound)	38720-5
Teacher's Edition	38726-4
*Skillpack Booklet	38731-0

Teacher's Edition of Skillpack Booklet	38743-4
Skillpack Spirit Duplication Masters (boxed set of 140)	38736-1
Studybook (Workbook)	38753-1
Teacher's Edition of Studybook	38759-0
Level 8 Test (pkg. of 25 booklets, manual, key)	38794-9
Manual with Key for Level 8 Test (separate)	38797-3
Unit Tests (12 Test booklets, 1 Class Record Sheet, 1 Unit Test Manual and Key)	
Form A	38767-1
Form B	38773-6
Booster Activities (1 pkg. of 44 Spirit Duplication Masters and Manual)	38748-5
Reading Progress Cards (pkg. of 100) for Levels 1-15	39499-6
Individual Skills Inventory Cards (pkg. of 100) for Levels 1-13	39501-1
Pupil Profile Card (pkg. of 100) for Levels 2-15	39496-1
Instructional Wall Charts	39784-7
Informal Reading Inventory for Levels 3-13	39480-5
Grade 2 Parent/Home Activity Sheets (16 pads, 24 sheets per pad)	39587-9
Grade 2 Parent/Home Newspaper (3 issues, pkgs. of 24 each)	39625-5

Level 9

MYSTERY SNEAKER (hardbound)	38809-0
Teacher's Edition	38814-7
*Skillpack Booklet	38820-1
Teacher's Edition of Skillpack Booklet	38831-7
Skillpack Spirit Duplication Masters (boxed set of 140)	38826-0
Studybook (Workbook)	38842-2
Teacher's Edition of Studybook	38847-3
Level 9 Test (pkg. of 25 booklets, manual, key)	38882-1
Manual with Key for Level 9 Test (separate)	38886-4
Unit Tests (12 Test booklets, 1 Class Record Sheet, 1 Unit Test Manual and Key)	
Form A	38856-2
Form B	38861-9
Booster Activities (1 pkg. of 45 Spirit Duplication Masters and Manual)	38837-6
Reading Progress Cards (pkg. of 100) for Levels 1-15	39499-6
Individual Skills Inventory Cards (pkg. of 100) for Levels 1-13	39501-1
Pupil Profile Card (pkg. of 100) for Levels 2-15	39496-1
Instructional Wall Charts	39790-1
Informal Reading Inventory for Levels 3-13	39480-5
Grade 3 Parent/Home Activity Sheets (16 pads, 24 sheets per pad)	39592-5
Grade 3 Parent/Home Newspaper (3 issues, pkgs. of 24 each)	39632-8

Appears in Teacher's Edition of text

Code
Number

Code
Number

The Ginn Reading Program Continued

Level 10

TEN TIMES ROUND (hardbound) ..	38896-1
Teacher's Edition	38903-8
*Skillpack Booklet	38908-9
Teacher's Edition of Skillpack Booklet	38919-4
Skillpack Spirit Duplication Masters (boxed set of 144)	38913-5
Studybook (Workbook)	38929-1
Teacher's Edition of Studybook	38935-6
Level 10 Test (pkg. of 25 booklets, manual, key)	38970-4
Manual with Key for Level 10 Test (separate)	38973-9
Unit Tests (12 Test booklets, 1 Class Record Sheet, 1 Unit Test Manual and Key)	
Form A	38942-9
Form B	38948-8
Booster Activities (1 pkg. of 43 Spirit Duplication Masters and Manual)	38924-0
Reading Progress Cards (pkg. of 100) for Levels 1-15	39499-6
Individual Skills Inventory Cards (pkg. of 100) for Levels 1-13	39501-1
Pupil Profile Card (pkg. of 100) for Levels 2-15	39496-1
Instructional Wall Charts	39796-0
Informal Reading Inventory for Levels 3-13	39480-5
Grade 3 Parent/Home Activity Sheets (16 pads, 24 sheets per pad)	39592-5
Grade 3 Parent/Home Newspaper (3 issues, pkgs. of 24 each)	39632-8

Level 11

BAREFOOT ISLAND (hardbound) ..	38985-2
Teacher's Edition	38990-9
*Skillpack Booklet	38996-8
Teacher's Edition of Skillpack Booklet	39008-7
Skillpack Spirit Duplication Masters (boxed set of 188)	39003-6
Studybook (Workbook)	39019-2
Teacher's Edition of Studybook	39024-9
Level 11 Test (pkg. of 25 booklets, manual, key)	39060-5
Manual with Key for Level 11 Test (separate)	39064-8
Mid-Level Test for Level 11 (pkg. of 25 booklets, manual, key)	39071-0
Manual with Key for Mid-Level Test for Level 11 (separate)	39074-5
Unit Test (12 Test booklets, 1 Class Record Sheet, 1 Unit Test Manual and Key)	
Form A	39033-8
Form B	39039-7
Booster Activities (1 pkg. of 64 Spirit Duplication Masters and Manual)	39013-3
Reading Progress Cards (pkg. of 100) for Levels 1-15	39499-6
Individual Skills Inventory Cards (pkg. of 100) for Levels 1-13	39501-1
Pupil Profile Card (pkg. of 100) for Levels 2-15	39496-1
Instructional Wall Charts	39801-0

Informal Reading Inventory for Levels 3-13	39480-5
Grade 4 Parent/Home Activity Sheets (16 pads, 24 sheets per pad)	39598-4
Grade 4 Parent/Home Newspaper (3 issues, pkgs. of 24 each)	39637-9

Level 12

RIDE THE SUNRISE (hardbound)...	39086-9
Teacher's Edition	39091-5
*Skillpack Booklet	39097-4
Teacher's Edition of Skillpack Booklet	39107-5
Skillpack Spirit Duplication Masters (boxed set of 188)	39102-4
Studybook (Workbook)	39118-0
Teacher's Edition of Studybook	39123-7
Level 12 Test (pkg. of 25 booklets, manual, key)	39159-8
Manual with Key for Level 12 Test (separate)	39163-6
Mid-Level Test for Level 12 (pkg. of 25 booklets, manual, key)	39170-9
Manual with Key for Mid-Level Test for Level 12 (separate)	39173-3
Unit Tests (12 Test booklets, 1 Class Record Sheet, 1 Unit Test Manual and Key)	
Form A	39132-6
Form B	39137-7
Booster Activities (1 pkg. of 58 Spirit Duplication Masters and Manual)	39112-1
Reading Progress Cards (pkg. of 100) for Levels 1-15	39499-6
Individual Skills Inventory Cards (pkg. of 100) for Levels 1-13	39501-1
Pupil Profile Card (pkg. of 100) for Levels 2-15	39496-1
Instructional Wall Charts	39806-1
Informal Reading Inventory for Levels 3-13	39480-5
Grade 5 Parent/Home Activity Sheets (16 pads, 24 sheets per pad)	39604-2
Grade 5 Parent/Home Newspaper (3 issues, pkgs. of 24 each)	39642-5

Level 13

FLIGHTS OF COLOR (hardbound)	39184-9
Teacher's Edition	39190-3
*Skillpack Booklet	39196-2
Teacher's Edition of Skillpack Booklet	39206-3
Skillpack Spirit Duplication Masters (boxed set of 188)	39201-2
Studybook (Workbook)	39218-7
Teacher's Edition of Studybook	39223-3
Level 13 Test (pkg. of 25 booklets, manual, key)	39260-8
Manual with Key for Level 13 Test (separate)	39263-2
Mid-Level Test for Level 13 (pkg. of 25 booklets, manual, key)	39270-5
Manual with Key for Mid-Level Test for Level 13 (separate)	39274-8
Unit Tests (12 Test booklets, 1 Class Record Sheet, 1 Unit Test Manaul and Key)	
Form A	39231-4
Form B	39236-5

*Appears in Teacher's Edition of text

The Ginn Reading Program Continued

Booster Activities (1 pkg. of 61 Spirit Duplication Masters and Manual)....	39213-6
Reading Progress Cards (pkg. of 100) for Levels 1-15	39499-6
Individual Skills Inventory Cards (pkg. of 100) for Levels 1-13	39501-1
Individual Skills Inventory Cards (pkg. of 100) for Levels 13-15	39504-6
Pupil Profile Card (pkg. of 100) for Levels 2-15	39496-1
Instructional Wall Charts	39813-4
Informal Reading Inventory for Levels 3-13...........	39480-5
Grade 6 Parent/Home Activity Sheets (16 pads, 24 sheets per pad)	39609-3
Grade 6 Parent/Home Newspaper (3 issues, pkgs. of 24 each)	39648-4

Level 14

GREEN SALAD SEASONS (hardbound)	39284-5
Teacher's Guide...........	39291-8
*Skillpack Booklet	39296-9
Teacher's Edition of Skillpack Booklet	39307-8
Skillpack Spirit Duplication Masters (boxed set of 126)	39301-9
Studybook (Workbook)	39317-5
Teacher's Edition of Studybook	39322-1
Level 14 Test (pkg. of 25 booklets, manual, key)	39335-3
Manual with Key for Level 14 Test (separate)	39333-7
Booster Activities (1 pkg. of 51 Spirit Duplication Masters and Manual)....	39312-4
Reading Progress Cards (pkg. of 100) for Levels 1-15	39499-6
Individual Skills inventory Cards (pkg. of 100) for Levels 13-15	39504-6
Pupil Profile Card (pkg. of 100) for Levels 2-15	39496-1

Level 15

CHAINS OF LIGHT (hardbound)	39356-6
Teacher's Guide...........	39361-2
*Skillpack Booklet	39366-3
Teacher's Edition of Skillpack Booklet	39378-7
Skillpack Spirit Duplication Masters (boxed set of 126)	39373-6
Studybook (Workbook)	39389-2
Teacher's Edition of Studybook	39394-9
Level 15 Test (pkg. of 25 booklets, manual, key)	39409-0
Manual with Key for Level 15 Test (separate)	39406-6
Booster Activities (1 pkg. of 51 Spirit Duplication Masters and Manual)....	39383-3
Reading Progress Cards (pkg. of 100) for Levels 1-15	39499-6
Individual Skills Inventory Cards (pkg. of 100) for Levels 13-15	39504-6
Pupil Profile Card (pkg. of 100) for Levels 2-15	39496-1

Supplementary Materials

Big Books

Level 1, ONE POTATO, TWO	39818-5
Level 2, LITTLE DOG LAUGHED	39823-1

Instructional Wall Charts

Level 2	39751-0
Level 3	39756-1
Level 4	39763-4
Level 5	39768-5
Level 6	39773-1
Level 7	39779-0
Level 8	39784-7
Level 9	39790-1
Level 10	39796-0
Level 11	39801-0
Level 12	39806-1
Level 13.............	39813-4

Ginn Word Enrichment Program/1979©

BOOK A LOOK AND LISTEN...........	35831-0
Teacher's Edition	35832-9
BOOK B CONSONANT SOUNDS AND SYMBOLS...........	35833-7
Teacher's Edition	35834-5
BOOK C VOWELS AND VARIANTS	35835-3
Teacher's Edition	35836-1
BOOK D MORE VOWELS AND VARIANTS ...	35838-8
Teacher's Edition	35839-6
BOOK E SOUNDS AND SYLLABLES	35841-8
Teacher's Edition...........	35842-6
BOOK F MORE SOUNDS AND SYLLABLES.	35843-4
Teacher's Edition	35844-2
BOOK G WORKING WITH WORDS...........	35845-0
Teacher's Edition	35846-9

My Picture Dictionary/1977©

Hardcover...........	31522-0

My Second Picture Dictionary/1976©

Hardcover...........	31523-9

Webster's Dictionaries

Webster's Elementary Dictionary (Hardcover) ...

	663-40914-4
Teacher's Guide...............	663-40916-0

Webster's Intermediate Dictionary (Hardcover) ...

	663-40918-7
Teacher's Guide...............	663-40920-9

Webster's High School Dictionary (Hardcover) ...

	663-40922-5
Teacher's Guide	663-40924-1

*Appears in Teacher's Edition of text

Code Number

Code Number

Webster's Dictionaries Continued

Webster's School
Thesaurus (Hardcover) ... 663-40931-4
Teacher's Guide 663-40934-9

Webster's New Collegiate
Dictionary 8th Edition
No. 8 Gray Lexotone 877-79408-1
No. 9 Red Linen Pyroxylin,
thumb-indexed................. 409-87779-4
No. 10 Brown Skivertex,
thumb-indexed................. 877-79410-3
Teacher's Guide............... 663-40928-4

Webster's Collegiate
Thesaurus
No. 69 Wheat Linen,
thumb-indexed................. 877-79069-8

Webster's New
Geographical Dictionary
No. 46 thumb-indexed 877-79446-4

Webster's New
Dictionary of Synonyms
No. 41 thumb-indexed 877-79241-0

Webster's Biographical
Dictionary
No. 43 thumb-indexed 443-87779-3

Webster's "Big 7"
Collegiate Dictionary
No. 14.................... 314-87779-7

Webster's Third New
International Dictionary
No. 1 thumb-indexed 877-79201-1

Reading 720: Rainbow Edition 1979/80©

Placement Materials

Initial Placement Test (pkg. of 36
booklets, manual, key)............... 33806-9
Initial Placement Test (Spirit
Duplication Masters), and 2 Manuals
with Key.................... 30869-0
Manual and Key for Initial
Placement Test (pkg. of 5)........... 30870-4

Specimen Sets

Specimen Set, Initial Placement Test 30875-5
Specimen Set, Mastery Tests for
Levels 1-13................. 30874-7
Specimen Set, Instructional
Management System Components 36661-5

Parental Involvement

Letters to Parents, 1 each for
Levels 2-4; 2 each for Levels
5-13. Spirit Duplication
Masters................... 37390-5

Beginning Reading Kit

Complete Kit: Adhesive and Tactile
Letters, Picture/Word Cards, 4 decks
of identical Concept Cards, Study
Prints, Geometric Shapes, Key
Character Cards, Display Board,
set of 60 Spirit Duplication Masters,
2 records, Teacher's Edition........... 36174-5

Beginning Reading Kit
components
available separately

Teacher's Edition 36175-3
Key Character Cards (pkg. of 26
different cards) 36635-6
Picture Word Cards (pkg. of 100
different cards) 36178-8
Concept Cards (set of 4 decks) 36649-6
Study Prints (pkg. of 20 illustrations
on 10 cards, with Teacher's Edition) 36181-8
Spirit Duplication Masters (boxed
set of 60 worksheets).................. 36182-6
Geometric Shapes (set of 144 shapes) 36380-2
Other Level 1 items are available for
replacement purposes. Call
800-848-9500

Conversion Kit

Users of Reading 720 Hello Morning!
Kit who wish to convert to the
Reading 720: Rainbow Edition
Beginning Reading Kit may do so
by purchasing the Conversion Kit
(includes Key Character Cards,
Geometric Shapes, and Teacher's
Edition) 36658-5

Level 1

READY FOR RAINBOWS
Write-in Text (consumable) 37000-0
Teacher's Edition 37003-5
Mastery Test (pkg. of 36, manual, key) 30632-9
Manual with Key for Level 1
Mastery Test (separate) 30633-7
Reading Progress Cards (pkg. of 100)
for Levels 1-13 30873-9
Individual Skills Inventory Cards
(pkg. of 100) for Levels 1-13 36397-7
Skills Pattern Book
130 self-contained activities for
Levels 1-13—includes "blueprints"
for assembling non-consumable
teaching aids using art supplied in
the 30-page Appendix.
(Paperbound) 37392-1
Resource Activity Book
229 games and manipulative
activities for Levels 1-13, with lists of
professional reference sources and
selected sources of children s
literature. (Paperbound) 30868-2

Level 2

A POCKETFUL OF SUNSHINE
Write-in Text (consumable) 37007-8
Teacher's Edition 37010-8
*Skilpak Booklet 36190-7
*Skilpak Spirit Duplication Masters
(boxed set of 110).................... 36191-5
Take-Home Booklets 1-8 (pkg. of
12 each of Booklets 1-8).............. 36189-3
My Phonics Practicebook. 36381-0
Teacher's Edition of My Phonics
Practice Book 36382-9
Big Book 36873-1
Level 2 Mastery Test (pkg. of 36
booklets, manual, key)............... 30659-0
Manual with Key for Level 2
Mastery Test (separate) 30660-4

*Appears in Teacher's Edition of text

Code Number

Code Number

Reading 720: Rainbow Edition Continued

Unit Criterion
Exercise Package (12 Criterion
Exercise Booklets, 2 Criterion
Exercise Record Sheets, 1
Criterion Exercise Manual 36195-8

*Booster
Activities (1 pkg. of 30 Spirit
Duplication Masters and Manual).... 36197-4

*Reading
Achievement Cards (pkg. of 36 cards) 32881-0

Reading Progress Cards (pkg. of
100) for Levels 1-13 30873-9

Individual Skills Inventory Cards
(pkg. of 100) for Levels 1-13 36397-7

Unit Decoding Pretests (Spirit
Duplication Masters) for Levels 2-5 30661-2

Basic Card Set I for Levels 2-4 32574-9

Letters to Parents, 1 each for
Levels 2-4; 2 each for Levels
5-13. Spirit Duplication
Masters 37390-5

Skills Pattern Book
130 self-contained activities for
Levels 1-13—includes "blueprints"
for assembling non-consumable
teaching aids using art supplied in
the 30-page Appendix.
(Paperbound) 37392-1

Resource Activity Book
229 games and manipulative
activities for Levels 1-13, with lists of
professional reference sources and
selected sources of children's
literature. (Paperbound) 30868-2

Level 3

A DUCK IS A DUCK (paperbound) . 37013-2

Teacher's Edition 37016-7

*Skilpak Booklet 36202-4

*Skilpak Spirit Duplicaton Masters
(boxed set of 46) 36203-2

Studybook (Workbook) 36200-8

Teacher's Edition of Studybook 36201-6

Oral Language Workshop for
Levels 3-5 (1 pkg. of 26 Spirit
Duplication Masters and Manual).... 37733-1

Teacher's Manual for
Oral Language Workshop 37737-4

Big Book 36875-8

Instructional Wall Charts 36852-9

Level 3 Mastery Test (pkg. of 36
text booklets, manual, key) 30674-4

Manual with Key for Level 3
Mastery Test (separate) 30675-2

Unit Criterion
Exercise Package (12 Criterion
Exercise Booklets, 2 Criterion
Exercise Record Sheets, 1 Criterion
Exercise Manual) 36206-7

*Booster
Activities (1 pkg. of 17 Spirit
Duplication Masters and Manual).... 36208-3

*Reading
Achievement Cards (pkg. of 36 cards) 32884-5

Unit Decoding Pretests (Spirit
Duplication Masters) for Levels 2-5 30661-2

Basic Card Set I for Levels 2-4 32574-9

Picture Maps for Levels 3 and 4 31322-8

Reading Progress Cards (pkg. of
100) for Levels 1-13 30873-9

Individual Skills Inventory Cards
(pkg. of 100) Levels 1-13 36397-7

Letters to Parents, 1 each for
Levels 2-4; 2 each for Levels
5-13. Spirit Duplication
Masters 37390-5

Skills Pattern Book
130 self-contained activities for
Levels 1-13—includes "blueprints"
for assembling non-consumable
teaching aids using art supplied in
the 30-page Appendix.
(Paperbound) 37392-1

Resource Activity Book
229 games and manipulative
activities for Levels 1-13, with lists of
professional reference sources and
selected sources of children's
literature. (Paperbound) 30868-2

Level 4

HELICOPTERS AND
GINGERBREAD (paperbound) 37019-1

Teacher's Edition 37022-1

*Skilpak Booklet 36214-8

*Skilpak Spirit Duplication Masters
(boxed set of 46) 36215-6

Studybook (Workbook) 36211-3

Teacher's Edition of Studybook 36212-1

Oral Language Workshop for
Levels 3-5 (1 pkg. of 26 Spirit
Duplication Masters and Manual).... 37733-1

Teacher's Manual for
Oral Language Workshop 37737-4

Instructional Wall Charts 36853-7

Level 4 Mastery Test (pkg. of 36
test booklets, manual, key) 30687-6

Manual with Key for Level 4 Mastery
Test (separate) 30688-4

Unit Criterion
Exercise Package (12 Criterion
Exercise Booklets, 2 Criterion
Exercise Record Sheets, 1 Criterion
Exercise Manual) 36603-8

*Booster
Activities (1 pkg. of 14 Spirit
Duplication Masters and Manual).... 36221-0

*Reading
Achievement Cards (pkg. of 36 Cards) 32888-8

Unit Decoding Pretests (Spirit
Duplication Masters) for Levels 2-5 30661-2

Basic Card Set I for Levels 2-4 32574-9

Picture Maps for Levels 3 and 4 31322-8

Reading Progress Cards (pkg. of 100)
for Levels 1-13 30873-9

Individual Skills Inventory Cards
(pkg. of 100) for Levels 1-13 36397-7

Letters to Parents, 1 each for
Levels 2-4; 2 each for Levels
5-13. Spirit Duplication Masters 37390-5

Skills Pattern Book
130 self-contained activities for
Levels 1-13—includes "blueprints"
for assembling non-consumable
teaching aids using art supplied in
the 30-page Appendix.
(Paperbound) 37392-1

*Appears in Teacher's Edition of text

Code
Number

Code
Number

Reading 720: Rainbow Edition Continued

Resource Activity Book
229 games and manipulative
activities for Levels 1-13, with lists of
professional reference sources and
selected sources of children's
literature. (Paperbound) 30868-2

Level 5

MAY I COME IN? (hardbound) 37026-4
Teacher's Edition 37029-9
*Skilpak Booklet 36226-1
*Skilpak Spirit Duplication Masters
(boxed set of 110) 36228-8
Studybook (Workbook) 36224-5
Teacher's Edition of Studybook ... 36225-3
Oral Language Workshop for
Levels 3-5 (1 pkg. of 26 Spirit
Duplication Masters and Manual).... 37733-1
Teacher's Manual for
Oral Language Workshop 37737-4
Instructional Wall Charts............. 36854-5
Level 5 Mastery Test (pkg. of 36
test booklets, manual, key) 30703-1
Manual with Key for Level 5 Mastery
Test (separate)...................... 30705-8
Unit Criterion
Exercise Package (12 Criterion
Exercise Booklets, 2 Criterion
Exercise Record Sheets, 1 Criterion
Exercise Manual) 36233-4
*Booster
Activities (1 pkg. of 40 Spirit
Duplication Masters and Manual).... 36235-0
*Reading
Achievement Cards (pkg. of 36 cards) 32892-6
Unit Decoding Pretests (Spirit
Duplication Masters) for Levels 2-5 30661-2
Basic Card Set II for Levels 5-6 32575-7
Reading Progress Cards (pkg. of
100) for Levels 1-13................... 30873-9
Individual Skills Inventory Cards
(pkg. of 100) for Levels 1-13 36397-7
Letters to Parents, 1 each for
Levels 2-4; 2 each for Levels 5-13.
Spirit Duplication Masters 37390-5
Skills Pattern Book
130 self-contained activities for
Levels 1-13—includes "blueprints"
for assembling non-consumable
teaching aids using art supplied in
the 30-page Appendix.
(Paperbound) 37392-1
Resource Activity Book
229 games and manipulative
activities for Levels 1-13, with lists of
professional reference sources and
selected sources of children's
literature. (Paperbound) 30868-2

Level 6

ONE TO GROW ON
(hardbound)........................... 37032-9
Teacher's Edition 37035-3
*Skilpak Booklet 36240-7
*Skilpak Spirit Duplication Masters
(boxed set of 126).................... 36241-5
Studybook (Workbook) 30712-0
Teacher's Edition of Studybook 30713-9

Oral Language Workshop for
Levels 6-7 (1 pkg. of 32 Spirit
Duplication Masters and Manual).... 37743-9
Teacher's Manual for
Oral Language Workshop 37746-3
Instructional Wall Charts............. 36855-3
Level 6 Mastery Test (pkg. of 36
test booklets, manual, key) 30722-8
Manual with Key for Level 6 Mastery
Test (separate)...................... 30723-6
Unit Criterion
Exercise Package (12 Criterion
Exercise Booklets, 2 Criterion
Exercise Record Sheets, 1 Criterion
Exercise Manual) 36246-6
*Booster
Activities (1 pkg. of 47 Spirit
Duplication Masters and Manual).... 36248-2
*Reading
Achievement Cards (pkg. of 36 cards) 32895-0
Unit Decoding Pretests (Spirit
Duplication Masters) for Levels 6-10 30724-4
Basic Card Set II for Levels 5-6 32575-7
Reading Progress Cards (pkg. of
100) for Levels 1-13................... 30873-9
Individual Skills Inventory Cards
(pkg. of 100) for Levels 1-13 36397-7
Letters to Parents, 1 each for
Levels 2-4; 2 each for Levels
5-13. Spirit Duplication Masters 37390-5
Skills Pattern Book
130 self-contained activities for
Levels 1-13—includes "blueprints"
for assembling non-consumable
teaching aids using art supplied in
the 30-page Appendix.
(Paperbound) 37392-1
Resource Activity Book
229 games and manipulative
activities for Levels 1-13, with lists of
professional reference sources and
selected sources of children's
literature. (Paperbound) 30868-2

Level 7

THE DOG NEXT DOOR AND
OTHER STORIES (hardbound) 37039-6
Teacher's Edition 37043-4
*Skilpak Booklet 36253-9
*Skilpak Spirit Duplication Masters
(boxed set of 139).................... 36254-7
Studybook (Workbook) 30730-9
Teacher's Edition of Workbook 30731-7
Oral Language Workshop for
Levels 6-7 (1 pkg. of 32 Spirit
Duplication Masters and Manual).... 37743-9
Teacher's Manual for
Oral Language Workshop 37746-3
Instructional Wall Charts............. 36856-1
Level 7 Mastery Test (pkg. of 36
test booklets, manual, key) 30739-2
Manual with key for Level 7 Mastery
Test (separate)...................... 30740-6
Unit Criterion
Exercise Package (12 Criterion
Exercise Booklets, 2 Criterion
Exercise Record Sheets, 1 Criterion
Exercise Manual) 36257-1
*Booster
Activities (1 pkg. of 48 Spirit
Duplication Masters and Manual) ... 36260-1

*Appears in Teacher's Edition of text

Code Number

Reading 720: Rainbow Edition Continued

*Reading
Achievement Cards (pkg. of 36 cards) 32898-5

Unit Decoding Pretests (Spirit
Duplication Masters) for Levels 6-10 30724-4

Reading Progress Cards (pkg. of
100) for Levels 1-13 30873-9

Individual Skills Inventory Cards
(pkg. of 100) for Levels 1-13 36397-7

Letters to Parents, 1 each for
Levels 2-4; 2 each for Levels
5-13. Spirit Duplication Masters 37390-5

Skills Pattern Book
130 self-contained activities for
Levels 1-13—includes "blueprints"
for assembling non-consumable
teaching aids using art supplied in
the 30-page Appendix.
(Paperbound) 37392-1

Resource Activity Book
229 games and manipulative
activities for Levels 1-13, with lists of
professional reference sources and
selected sources of children's
literature. (Paperbound) 30868-2

Level 8

HOW IT IS NOWADAYS (hardbound) 37046-9

Teacher's Edition 37049-3

*Skilpak Booklet 36266-0

*Skilpak Spirit Duplication Masters
(boxed set of 142) 36267-9

Studybook (Workbook) 30747-3

Teacher's Edition of Studybook 30748-1

Oral Language Workshop for
Levels 8-9 (1 pkg. of 32 Spirit
Duplication Masters and Manual) 37754-4

Teacher's Manual for
Oral Language Workshop 37757-9

Instructional Wall Charts 36858-8

*Level 8 Mastery Test (pkg. of 36
test booklets, manual, key) 30757-0

Manual with Key for Level 8 Mastery
Test (separate) 30758-9

Unit Criterion
Exercise Package (12 Criterion
Exercise Booklets, 2 Criterion
Exercise Record Sheets, 1 Criterion
Exercise Manual) 36270-9

*Booster
Activities (1 pkg. of 44 Spirit
Duplication Masters and Manual) 36272-5

*Reading
Achievement Cards (pkg. of 36 cards) 32901-9

Unit Decoding Pretests (Spirit
Duplication Masters) for Level 6-10 30724-4

Reading Progress Cards (pkg. of
100) for Levels 1-13 30873-9

Individual Skills Inventory Cards
(pkg. of 100) for Levels 1-13 36397-7

Letters to Parents, 1 each for
Levels 2-4; 2 each for Levels
5-13. Spirit Duplication
Masters 37390-5

Skills Pattern Book
130 Self-contained activities for
Levels 1-13—includes "blueprints"
for assembling non-consumable
teaching aids using art supplied in
the 30-page Appendix.
(Paperbound) 37392-1

Code Number

Resource Activity Book
229 games and manipulative
activities for Levels 1-13, with lists of
professional reference sources and
selected sources of children's
literature. (Paperbound) 30868-2

Level 9

INSIDE OUT (hardbound) 37052-3

Teacher's Edition 37056-6

*Skilpak Booklet 36278-4

*Skilpak Spirit Duplication Masters
(boxed set of 108) 36279-2

Studybook (Workbook) 30765-1

Teacher's Edition of Studybook 30767-8

Oral Language Workshop for
Levels 8-9 (1 pkg. of 32 Spirit
Duplication Masters) 37754-4

Teacher's Manual for
Oral Language Workshop 37757-9

Instructional Wall Charts 36859-6

Level 9 Mastery Test (pkg. of 36
test booklets, manual, key) 30773-2

Manual with Key for Level 9 Mastery
Test (separate) 30774-0

Unit Criterion
Exercise Package (12 Criterion
Exercise Booklets, 2 Criterion
Exercise Record Sheets, 1 Criterion
Exercise Manual) 36282-2

*Booster
Activities (1 pkg. of 40 Spirit
Duplication Masters and Manual) 36284-9

*Reading
Achievement Cards (pkg. of 36 cards) 32904-3

Unit Decoding Pretests (Spirit
Duplication Masters) for Levels 6-10 30724-4

Reading Progress Cards (pkg. of
100) for Levels 1-13 30873-9

Individual Skills Inventory Cards
(pkg. of 100) for Levels 1-13 36397-7

Letters to Parents, 1 each for
Levels 2-4; 2 each for Levels
5-13. Spirit Duplication
Masters 37390-5

Skills Pattern Book
130 self-contained activities for
Levels 1-13—includes "blueprints"
for assembling non-consumable
teaching aids using art supplied in
the 30-page Appendix.
(Paperbound) 37392-1

Resource Activity Book
229 games and manipulative
activities for Levels 1-13, with lists of
professional reference sources and
selected sources of children's
literature. (Paperbound) 30868-2

Level 10

A LIZARD TO START WITH
(hardbound) 37059-0

Teacher's Edition 37062-0

*Skilpak Booklet 36293-8

*Skilpak Spirit Duplication Masters
(boxed set of 142) 36294-6

Studybook (Workbook) 30787-2

Teacher's Edition of Studybook 30788-0

Oral Language Workshop for
Level 10 (1 pkg. of 62 Spirit
Duplication Masters and Manual) 37763-3

*Appears in Teacher's Edition of text

Code Number

Reading 720: Rainbow Edition Continued

Teacher's Manual for
Oral Language Workshop 37767-6

Instructional Wall Charts............... 36861-8

Level 10 Mastery Test (pkg. of 36
test booklets, manual, key) 30794-5

Manual with Key for Level 10
Mastery Test (separate) 30795-3

Unit Criterion
Exercise Package (12 Criterion
Exercise Booklets, 2 Criterion
Exercise Record Sheets, 1 Criterion
Exercise Manual) 36297-0

*Booster
Activities (1 pkg. of 40 Spirit
Duplication Masters and Manual).... 36299-7

*Reading
Achievement Cards (pkg. of 36 cards) 32908-6

Unit Decoding Pretests (Spirit
Duplication Masters) for Levels 6-10 30724-4

Reading Progress Cards (pkg. of
100) for Levels 1-13 30873-9

Individual Skills Inventory Cards
(pkg. of 100) for Levels 1-13 36397-7

Letters to Parents, 1 each for
Levels 2-4; 2 each for Levels
5-13. Spirit Duplication
Masters 37390-5

Skills Pattern Book
130 self-contained activities for
Levels 1-13—includes "blueprints"
for assembling non-consumable
teaching aids using art supplied in
the 30-page Appendix.
(Paperbound) 37392-1

Resource Activity Book
229 games and manipulative
activities for Levels 1-13, with lists of
professional reference sources and
selected sources of children's
literature. (Paperbound) 30868-2

Level 11

TELL ME HOW THE SUN ROSE
(hardbound)............................. 37065-5

Teacher's Edition 37069-8

*Skilpak Booklet 36324-1

*Skilpak Spirit Duplication Masters
(boxed set of 174)...................... 36326-8

Studybook (Workbook) 30809-7

Teacher's Edition of Studybook 30810-0

Oral Language Workshop for
Level 11 (1 pkg. of 62 Spirit
Duplication Masters and Manual).... 37773-0

Teacher's Manual for
Oral Language Workshop 37776-5

Instructional Wall Charts............... 37523-1

Level 11 Mastery Test (pkg. of 36
test booklets, manual, key) 30817-8

Manual with Key for Level 11
Mastery Test (separate) 30818-6

Unit Criterion
Exercise Package (12 Criterion
Exercise Booklets, 2 Criterion
Exercise Record Sheets, 1 Criterion
Exercise Manual) 36329-2

*Booster
Activities (1 pkg. of 35 Spirit
Duplication Masters and Manual).... 36331-4

Code Number

*Reading
Achievement Cards (pkg. of 36 cards) 32911-6

Reading Progress Cards (pkg. of
100) for Levels 1-13..................... 30873-9

Individual Skills Inventory Cards
(pkg. of 100) for Levels 1-13 36397-7

Letters to Parents, 1 each for
Levels 2-4; 2 each for Levels
5-13. Spirit Duplication
Masters 37390-5

Skills Pattern Book
130 self-contained activities for
Levels 1-13—includes "blueprints"
for assembling non-consumable
teaching aids using art supplied in
the 30-page Appendix.
(Paperbound) 37392-1

Resource Activity Book
229 games and manipulative
activities for Levels 1-13, with lists of
professional reference sources and
selected sources of children's
literature. (Paperbound) 30868-2

Level 12

MEASURE ME, SKY (hardbound) ... 37073-6

Teacher's Edition 37076-0

*Skilpak Booklet 36338-1

*Skilpak Spirit Duplication Masters
(boxed set of 158)...................... 36340-3

Studybook (Workbook) 30830-5

Teacher's Edition of Studybook 30831-3

Oral Language Workshop for
Level 12 (1 pkg. of 32 Spirit
Duplication Masters and Manual).... 37784-6

Teacher's Manual for
Oral Language Workshop 37787-0

Instructional Wall Charts............... 37525-8

Level 12 Mastery Test (pkg. of 36
test booklets, manual, key) 30838-0

Manual with Key for Level 12
Mastery Test (separate) 30839-9

Unit Criterion
Exercise Package (12 Criterion
Exercise Booklets, 2 Criterion
Exercise Record Sheets, 1 Criterion
Exercise Manual) 36344-6

*Booster
Activities (1 pkg. of 36 Spirit
Duplication Masters and Manual).... 36346-2

*Reading
Achievement Cards (pkg. of 36 cards) 32914-0

Reading Progress Cards (pkg. of
100) for Levels 1-13..................... 30873-9

Individual Skills Inventory Cards
(pkg. of 100) for Levels 1-13 36397-7

Letters to Parents, 1 each for
Levels 2-4; 2 each for Levels
5-13. Spirit Duplication
Masters 37390-5

Skills Pattern Book
130 self-contained activities for
Levels 1-13—includes "blueprints"
for assembling non-consumable
teaching aids using art supplied in
the 30-page Appendix.
(Paperbound) 37392-1

*Appears in Teacher's Edition of text

	Code Number

Reading 720: Rainbow Edition Continued

Resource Activity Book
229 games and manipulative
activities for Levels 1-13, with lists of
professional reference sources and
selected sources of children's
literature. (Paperbound) 30868-2

Level 13

MOUNTAINS ARE FOR CLIMBING
(hardbound)............................. 37079-5
Teacher's Edition 37082-5
*Skilpak Booklet 36353-5
*Skilpak Spirit Duplication Masters
(boxed set of 190)...................... 36354-3
Studybook (Workbook) 30853-4
Teacher's Edition of Studybook 30854-2
Oral Language Workshop for
Level 13 (1 pkg. of 32 Spirit
Duplication Masters and Manual).... 37793-5
Teacher's Manual for
Oral Language Workshop 37797-8
Instructional Wall Charts.............. 37526-6
Level 13 Mastery Test (pkg. of 36
test booklets, manual, key) 30860-7
Manual with Key for Level 13
Mastery Test (separate) 30861-5
Unit Criterion
Exercise Package (12 Criterion
Exercise Booklets, 2 Criterion
Exercise Record Sheets, 1 Criterion
Exercise Manual) 36358-6
*Booster
Activities (1 pkg. of 33 Spirit
Duplication Masters and Manual).... 36360-8
*Reading
Achievement Cards (pkg. of 36 cards) 32917-5
Reading Progress Cards (pkg. of
100) for Levels 1-13 30873-9
Individual Skills Inventory Cards
(pkg. of 100) for Levels 1-13 36397-7
Letters to Parents, 1 each for
Levels 2-4; 2 each for Levels
5-13. Spirit Duplication
Masters 37390-5
Skills Pattern Book
130 self-contained activities for
Levels 1-13—includes "blueprints"
for assembling non-consumable
teaching aids using art supplied in
the 30-page Appendix.
(Paperbound) 37392-1
Resource Activity Book
229 games and manipulative
activities for Levels 1-13, with lists of
professional reference sources and
selected sources of children's
literature. (Paperbound) 30868-2

Reading 720: Rainbow Edition
Levels 14 and 15/1980©

Level 14

WINDOWS AND WALLS
(hardbound)............................. 37495-2
Teacher's Guide 37496-0
*Skilpak Booklet 37498-7
*Skilpak Spirit Duplication Masters
(boxed set of 126)...................... 37497-9

	Code Number

Studybook (Workbook) 37582-7
Teacher's Edition of Studybook 37583-5
Mastery Test (pkg. of 36 test
booklets, manual, key) 37584-3
Manual with Key for Mastery Test
(separate) 37585-1

Level 15

ORBITS AND OPPORTUNITIES
(hardbound) 37499-5
Teacher's Guide......................... 37500-2
*Skilpak Booklet 37502-9
*Skilpak Spirit Duplication Masters
(boxed set of 126)...................... 37501-0
Studybook (Workbook) 37587-8
Teacher's Edition of Studybook 37588-6
Mastery Test (pkg. of 36 test
booklets, manual, key)................. 37589-4
Manual with Key for Mastery Test
(separate) 37590-8

Reading 720/1978©

For students who need extra practice in basic reading skills.

Level 14A

TO MAKE A DIFFERENCE
(hardbound)............................. 35413-7
Teacher's Guide (includes students'
skills activities and unit tests) 35414-5
*Skilpak Booklet 36791-3
*Skilpak Spirit Duplication Masters
(boxed set of 84) 36730-1
Studybook (Workbook) 35415-3
Teacher's Edition of Studybook 35416-1

Level 15A

GIFTS OF PROMISE (hardcover) ... 35418-8
Teacher's Guide (includes students'
skills activities and unit tests) 35419-6
*Skilpak Booklet 36792-1
*Skilpak Spirit Duplication Masters
(boxed set of 84) 36732-8
Studybook (Workbook) 35421-8
Teacher's Edition of Studybook 35422-6

Supplementary Materials
Instructional Wall Charts

Level 3 36852-9
Level 4 36853-7
Level 5 36854-5
Level 6 36855-3
Level 7 36856-1
Level 8 36858-8
Level 9 36859-6
Level 10................................... 36861-8
Level 11................................... 37523-1
Level 12................................... 37525-8
Level 13................................... 37526-6

Big Books

Level 2, POCKETFUL OF
SUNSHINE BIG BOOK................ 36873-1

*Appears in Teacher's Edition of text

Code
Number

Reading 720: Rainbow Edition

Level 3, A DUCK IS A DUCK
BIG BOOK.......................... 36875-8

Skills Pattern Book

130 self-contained activities for
Levels 1-13—includes "blueprints"
for assembling non-consumable
teaching aids using art supplied in
the 30-page Appendix.
(Paperbound)............................ 37392-1

Resource Activity Book

229 games and manipulative
activities for Levels 1-13, with lists of
professional reference sources and
selected sources of children's
literature. (Paperbound) 30868-2

Readalong Recordings

Level 3, A Duck Is a Duck (1 record)   36877-4

Level 4, Helicopters and Ginger-
bread (1 record) 36878-2

Level 5, May I Come In? (2 records)   36879-0

Level 6, One to Grow On (3 records)   36882-0

Level 7, The Dog Next Door and
Other Stories (3 records)............... 36886-3

Decoding Activity Charts

DECODING ACTIVITY CHARTS A
(Reading 360 and Reading 720,
Levels K-1) (8 charts, manipulative
pieces, Teacher's Guide)........... 25290-3

Teacher's Guide (separate)........... 25066-8

DECODING ACTIVITY CHARTS B
(Reading 360 and Reading 720,
Levels 2-6) (14 charts, manipulative
pieces, Teacher's Guide).............. 25291-1

Teacher's Guide (separate)........... 25120-6

DECODING ACTIVITY CHARTS C
(Reading 360 and Reading 720,
Levels 7-8) (12 charts, manipulative
pieces, Teacher's Guide).............. 25293-8

Teacher's Guide (separate) 25127-3

DECODING ACTIVITY CHARTS D
(Reading 360 and Reading 720,
Levels 9-10) (10 charts,
manipulative pieces, Teacher's
Guide) 25294-6

Teacher's Guide (separate)........... 25136-2

SAVE 10% Purchase all four sets
including Teacher's Guides 36696-8

Supplementary Materials Bibliography Cards

Suggestions for books and anthol-
ogies for each unit and level, audio-
visual aids, professional materials,
directory of publishers................ 32962-0

My Phonics Practice Book

Write-in Text for additional practice
and reinforcement in decoding skills   36381-0

Teacher's Edition of My Phonics
Practice Book 36382-9

Reading 720: Tutorial/1980©

Supervisor's Manual.................... 40370-7

Tutor's Guide 40375-8

Accessory Package 40387-1

Levels 2-5 Kit............................. 40393-6

Levels 6 and 7 Kit....................... 40397-9

Ginn Word Enrichment Program/1979©

BOOK A
LOOK AND LISTEN.................... 35831-0

Teacher's Edition 35832-9

BOOK B
CONSONANTS SOUNDS AND
SYMBOLS 35833-7

Teacher's Edition 35834-5

BOOK C
VOWELS AND VARIANTS 35835-3

Teacher's Edition 35836-1

BOOK D
MORE VOWELS AND VARIANTS... 35838-8

Teacher's Edition 35839-6

BOOK E
SOUNDS AND SYLLABLES 35841-8

Teacher's Edition....................... 35842-6

BOOK F
MORE SOUNDS AND SYLLABLES. 35843-4

Teacher's Edition 35844-2

BOOK G
WORKING WITH WORDS............. 35845-0

Teacher's Edition 35846-9

Magic Circle Books

Complete Magic Circle Collection

Save nearly $200. Buy the complete
collection—five copies each of 90
titles ($769.95 if all components
are purchased separately) 36693-3

Complete Library Units

Levels 1 and 2 Complete Library
Unit (5 copies of each title,
Teacher's Guide, 5 copies of the
Skill Card for each title, 2 copies
of the Spirit Duplication Master
for each level) 30925-5

Levels 3 and 4 Complete Library
Unit (5 copies of each title,
Teacher's Guide, 5 copies of the
Skill Card for each title, 2 copies
of the Spirit Duplication Master
for each level) 30926-3

Level 5 Complete Library Unit
(5 copies of each title, Teacher's
Guide, 5 copies of the Skill Card for
each title, 2 copies of the Spirit
Duplication Master) 30927-1

Level 6 Complete Library Unit
(5 copies of each title, Teacher's
Guide, 5 copies of the Skill Card
for each title, 2 copies of the Spirit
Duplication Master) 30929-8

Level 7 Complete Library Unit
(5 copies of each title, Teacher's
Guide, 5 copies of the Skill Card for
each title, 2 copies of the Spirit
Duplication Master) 30930-1

Level 8 Complete Library Unit
(5 copies of each title, Teacher's
Guide, 5 copies of the Skill Card for
each title, 2 copies of the Spirit
Duplication Master) 30932-8

Code
Number

Magic Circle Books Continued

Level 9 Complete Library Unit
(5 copies of each title, Teacher's
Guide, 5 copies of the Skill Card for
each title, 2 copies of the Spirit
Duplication Master) 30933-6

Level 10 Complete Library Unit
(5 copies of each title, Teacher's
Guide, 5 copies of the Skill Card for
each title, 2 copies of the Spirit
Duplication Master) 30934-4

Magic Circle Components Available separately

To accompany Levels 1 and 2

Levels 1 and 2—Package (1 each of
8 titles, Teacher's Guide) 24839-6
Teacher's Guide (separate) 24851-5
Skill Cards (5 copies of each title) ... 30560-8
Spirit Duplication Masters (2 copies
for each level) 30917-4
INDIVIDUAL TITLES (in pkgs. of 5)
We Need a Bigger Zoo! (Bunting).... 24844-2
Walk, Robot, Walk (Mayer) 24841-8
Small Garden—Big Surprise (Adkins) 24843-4
The Bumbershoot (Hammond,
Winslow) 24842-6
Run! (Lane) 24847-7
Ride, Ride, Ride (Wiesbauer) 24849-3
Hide (Martin) 24848-5
The Park—The Park (Freschet) 24850-7

To accompany Levels 3 and 4

Levels 3 and 4—Package (1 each of
12 titles, Teacher's Guide) 24852-3
Teacher's Guide (separate) 24866-3
Skill Cards (5 copies for each title) .. 30561-6
Spirit Duplication Masters (2 copies
for each level) 30918-2
INDIVIDUAL TITLES (in pkgs. of 5)
Jill (Wiesbauer) 24853-1
Stop! Look! (Maynard) 24858-2
Cat (Martin) 24857-4
Duck in the Park/Duck in the Dark
(Begley) 24856-6
Where Is Zip? (Robison) 24859-0
Look with May Ling (Maxwell) 24855-8
How Can You Hide an Elephant?
(Martin) 24860-4
Do You See a Mouse? (Crume) 24861-2
The Pine Park Team (Seymour) 24862-0
"What Is It?" Said the Dog (Allen) ... 24865-5
In The Zoo (Lane) 24864-7
Inside the Red and White Tent
(Jensen) 24863-9

To accompany Level 5

Level 5—Package (1 each of 11 titles,
Teacher's Guide) 24867-1
Teacher's Guide (separate) 24880-9
Skill Cards (5 copies for each title) .. 30562-4
Spirit Duplication Master (2 copies
for the level) 30919-0
INDIVIDUAL TITLES (in pkgs. of 5,
except Blue Skies Magic)
Here Comes Pops (Wong) 24870-1

Code
Number

Tom Turtle (Hill) 24869-8
Say It Fast (Bunting) 24873-6
From My Window (Wong) 24872-8
The Big Green Bean (Wiesbauer).... 24879-5
Box, Fox, Ox, and the Peacock
(Bunting).................................. 24875-2
Said the Little Raccoon to the Moon
(Morton)................................... 24876-0
Imagine That! (Fife) 24874-4
The Little Elephant Who Liked to Play
(Sellers) 24877-9
The Tail of the Mouse (Lexau) 24878-7
*Blue Skies Magic (Green) 29159-3
*(Not available in packages of 5.)

To accompany Level 6

Level 6—Package (1 each of 12 titles,
Teacher's Guide)......................... 24933-3
Teacher's Guide (separate)............ 29816-4
Skill Cards (5 copies for each title) .. 30563-2
Spirit Duplication Masters (2 copies
for the level) 30920-4
INDIVIDUAL TITLES (in pkgs. of 5)
Boy in the Middle (Bond) 25393-4
Nine on a String (Bade) 25394-2
Paint Me a Picture, Mr. Pine (Kessler) 25395-0
The Nothing Zoo (Bohoy) 25396-9
The Pet Show (A. Johnson) 25397-7
Lines Make Me Lonely (Madian) 25398-5
Angel the Pig (Clapman)............... 25399-3
The Glerp (McPhail)..................... 25400-0
Monsters that Move Earth
(R. Johnson) 25401-9
Kim Ann and the Yellow Machine
(Palmer) 25402-7
The Wind and the Sun (de Paola) 25403-5
Monkey's Tail/Rabbit's Cup (Turner) 25404-3

To accompany Level 7

Level 7—Package (1 each of 11 titles,
Teacher's Guide)......................... 24881-7
Teacher's Guide (separate)............ 29817-2
Skill Cards (5 copies for each title) .. 30564-0
Spirit Duplication Master (2 copies
for the level) 30921-2
INDIVIDUAL TITLES (in pkgs. of 5)
Yesterday I Lost a Sneaker (McPhail) 24882-5
William's Dog (Martin) 24883-3
Zoo Babies (Morton) 24884-1
The Opossum's Table (Hinckely) 24886-8
Dancing Nadine (Clapman) 24887-6
Tuloose the Miserable Moose
(Hickox) 24888-4
Blast Off (Cain, Rosenbaum) 24889-2
Oliver Twister and His Big Little
Sister (Yeo)............................... 24891-4
Joey Tigertail (Comfort) 24892-2
Old Lion and His Friends (Brandt) ... 24893-0
Prince Littlefoot (Freschet) 24894-9

To accompany Level 8

Level 8—Package (1 each of 12 titles,
Teacher's Guide)......................... 24934-1
Teacher's Guide (separate)........... 29818-0
Skill Cards (5 copies for each title) .. 30565-9
Spirit Duplication Master (2 copies
for the level) 30922-0

*Appears in Teacher's Edition of text

Code Number

Code Number

Magic Circle Books Continued

INDIVIDUAL TITLES (in pkgs. of 5)
The King, the Dragon, and the Witch (Corsi) 25405-1

The House on the Top of the Hill (Daem) 25407-8

The Magic Donkey (Joyce) 25408-6

A Horse for Matthew Allen (Smiley) . 25409-4

The Long Line of Letters (Bartholomew) 25410-8

The Wonder of Change (Milgrom) ... 25411-6

So Many Henrys (Schatz) 25412-4

The Soapsuds Fairy (Palmer) 25413-2

The Moon—Jack and Jill and Other Legends (Branley) 25414-0

Through a Magic Glass (Russell) 25415-9

In a Time Long Past (Brandt) 25416-7

The Two Giants (Bunting) 25417-5

To accompany Level 9

Level 9—Package (1 each of 12 titles, Teacher's Guide) 24896-5

Teacher's Guide (separate) 29819-9

Skill Cards (5 copies for each title) .. 30566-7

Spirit Duplication Master (2 copies for the level) 30923-9

INDIVIDUAL TITLES (in pkgs. of 5)
Mystery of the Blue Condor (Arden) 24897-3

Joey's Secret (McCracken) 24898-1

Robbie of the Kirkhaven Team (Rowland) 24900-7

A Gift for Lonny (Bunting) 24901-5

The Haganinny (Anderson) 24902-3

Jokes, Jests, and Jollies (Hoke) 24903-1

The Future Explorers' Club (Bendick) 24972-4

The Great Moon Hoax (Branley) 24905-8

The Runaway Camper (Conley) 24906-6

Susi Did It (R. Johnson) 24908-2

The Unicorn and the Moon (de Paola) 24909-0

The Valiant Little Potter (Berry) 24910-4

To accompany Level 10

Level 10—Package (1 each of 12 titles, Teacher's Guide) 22992-8

Teacher's Guide (separate) 29820-2

Skill Card (5 copies of each title) 30567-5

Spirit Duplication Master (2 copies for the level) 30924-7

INDIVIDUAL TITLES (in pkgs. of 5)
Small Paul and the Bully of Morgan Court (Horvath) 25418-3

No One Need Ever Know (Read) 25419-1

Spring Is in the Air (Smith) 25420-5

School on a Raft (Beattie) 25421-3

The Dragon with a Thousand Wrinkles (Daem) 25422-1

Mags (Maclean) 25424-8

Beaver Boy (Dueland) 25425-6

The Circus Detectives (Abels) 25426-4

The Pine Tree that Went to Sea (Dueland) 25427-2

Dinosaur Dan (Reinstedt) 25428-0

The Troubles of Kings: Two Tales from Africa (Schatz) 25429-9

The Miller King (Tashjan) 25430-2

My Picture Dictionary/1977©

Hardcover 31522-0

My Second Picture Dictionary/1976©

Hardcover 31523-9

Webster's Dictionaries

Webster's Elementary Dictionary (Hardcover) ... 663-40914-4

Teacher's Guide 663-40916-0

Webster's Intermediate Dictionary (Hardcover) ... 663-40918-7

Teacher's Guide 663-40920-9

Reading 720/1976©

Placement Materials

Initial Placement Test (pkg. of 36 booklets, manual, key) 33806-9

Initial Placement Test (Spirit Duplication Masters), and 2 Manuals with Key 30869-0

Manual and Key for Initial Placement Test (pkg. of 5) 30870-4

Specimen Sets

Specimen Set, Initial Placement Test 30875-5

Specimen Set, Mastery Test for Levels 1-13 30874-7

Specimen Set, Instructional Management System Components .. 30876-3

Parental Involvement

Letters to Parents, 1 each for Levels 2-4; 2 each for Levels 5-13. Spirit Duplication Masters 37390-5

Level 1 Kit materials available separately

Level 1 Mastery Test (pkg. of 36, manual, key) 30632-9

Manual with Key for Level 1 Mastery Test (separate) 30633-7

Reading Progress Cards (pkg. of 100) for Levels 1-13 30873-9

Individual Skills Inventory Cards (pkg. of 100) for Levels 1-13 36397-7

Level 1

HELLO, MORNING!
Write-in Text
This prereading program of language concepts, letter discrimination, and phoneme-grapheme correspondences for initial consonants can be used alone or in conjunction with the HELLO, MORNING! Kit.

Write-in Text (consumable) 30630-2

Teacher's Edition 30631-0

Level 2

A POCKETFUL OF SUNSHINE (paperbound) 30634-5

	Code Number

Reading 720 Continued

Teacher's Edition	30635-3
*Skilpak Booklet	30650-7
*Skilpak Spirit Duplication Masters (pkg. of 94)	33270-2
Take-Home Booklets 1-8 (pkg. of 12 each of Booklets 1-8)	33074-2
Level 2 Mastery Test (pkg. of 36, manual, key)	30659-0
Manual with Key for Level 2 Mastery Test (separate)	30660-4
*Management System Criterion Exercise Package (12 Criterion Exercise Booklets, 2 Criterion Exercise Record Sheets, 1 Criterion Exercise Manual)	32879-9
*Management System Booster Activities (1 pkg. of 30 Spirit Duplication Masters and Manual)	30664-7
*Management System Reading Achievement Cards (pkg. of 36 Cards)	32881-0
Unit Decoding Pretests (Spirit Duplication Masters) for Levels 2-5	30661-2
Basic Card Set I for Levels 2-4	32574-9
Reading Progress Cards (pkg. of 100) for Levels 1-13	30873-9
Individual Skills Inventory Cards (pkg. of 100) for Levels 1-13	36397-7
Letters to Parents	37390-5

Level 3

A DUCK IS A DUCK (paperbound)	30665-5
Teacher's Edition	30666-3
*Skilpak Booklet	30670-1
*Skilpak Spirit Duplication Masters (pkg. of 46)	33271-0
Studybook (Workbook)	30667-1
Teacher's Edition of Studybook	30669-8
Instructional Wall Charts	36734-4
Level 3 Mastery Test (pkg. of 36, manual, key)	30674-4
Manual with Key for Level 3 Mastery Test (separate)	30675-2
*Management System Criterion Exercise Package (12 Criterion Exercise Booklets, 2 Criterion Exercise Record Sheets, 1 Criterion Exercise Manual)	32882-9
*Management System Booster Activities (1 pkg. of 17 Spirit Duplication Masters and Manual)	30679-5
*Management System Reading Achievement Cards (pkg. of 36 Cards)	32884-5
Picture Maps for Levels 3 and 4	31322-8
Unit Decoding Pretests (Spirit Duplication Masters) for Levels 2-5	30661-2
Basic Card Set I for Levels 2-4	32574-9
Reading Progress Cards (pkg. of 100) for Levels 1-13	30873-9
Individual Skills Inventory Card (pkg. of 100) for Levels 1-13	36397-7
Letters to Parents	37390-5

Level 4

HELICOPTERS AND GINGERBREAD (paperbound)	30680-9

	Code Number
Teacher's Edition	31521-2
*Skilpak Booklet	30683-3
*Skilpak Spirit Duplication Masters (boxed set of 46)	33272-9
Studybook (Workbook)	30681-7
Teacher's Edition of Studybook	30682-5
Instructional Wall Charts	36735-2
Level 4 Mastery Test (pkg. of 36 test booklets, manual, key)	30687-6
Manual with Key for Level 4 Mastery Test (separate)	30688-4
*Management System Criterion Exercise Package (12 Criterion Exercise Booklets, 2 Criterion Exercise Record Sheets, 1 Criterion Exercise Manual)	32885-3
*Management System Booster Activities (1 pkg. of 14 Spirit Duplication Masters and Manual)	30692-2
*Management System Reading Achievement Cards (pkg. of 36 Cards)	32888-8
Picture Maps for Levels 3 and 4	31322-8
Unit Decoding Pretests (Spirit Duplication Masters) for Levels 2-5	30661-2
Basic Cards Set I for Levels 2-4	32574-9
Reading Progress Cards (pkg. of 100) for Levels 1-13	30873-9
Individual Skills Inventory Card (pkg. of 100) for Levels 1-13	36397-7
Letters to Parents	37390-5

Level 5

MAY I COME IN? (hardbound)	30693-0
Teacher's Edition	30694-9
*Skilpak Booklet	30697-3
*Skilpak Spirit Duplication Masters (boxed set of 110)	33273-7
Studybook (Workbook)	30695-7
Teacher's Edition of Studybook	30696-5
Instructional Wall Charts	36736-0
Level 5 Mastery Test (pkg. of 36 test booklets, manual, key)	30703-1
Manual with Key for Level 5 Mastery Test (separate)	30705-8
*Management System Criterion Exercise Package (12 Criterion Exercise Booklets, 2 Criterion Exercise Record Sheets, 1 Criterion Exercise Manual)	32889-6
*Management System Booster Activities (1 pkg. of 40 Spirit Duplication Masters and Manual)	30709-0
*Management System Reading Achievement Cards (pkg. of 36 cards)	32892-6
Unit Decoding Pretests (Spirit Duplication Masters) for Levels 2-5	30661-2
Basic Card Set II for Levels 5-6	32575-7
Reading Progress Cards (pkg. of 100) for Levels 1-13	30873-9
Individual Skills Inventory Cards (pkg. of 100) for Levels 1-13	36397-7
Letters to Parents	37390-5

Level 6

ONE TO GROW ON (hardbound)	30710-4
Teacher's Edition	30711-2

*Appears in Teacher's Edition of text

Code
Number

Reading 720 Continued

*Skilpak Booklet	30714-7
*Skilpak Spirit Duplication Masters (boxed set of 126)	33274-5
Studybook (Workbook)	30712-0
Teacher's Edition of Studybook	30713-9
Instructional Wall Charts	36737-9
Level 6 Mastery Test (pkg. of 36 test booklets, manual, key)	30722-8
Manual with Key for Level 6 Mastery Test (separate)	30723-6
*Management System Criterion Exercise Package (12 Criterion Exercise Booklets, 2 Criterion Exercise Record Sheets, 1 Criterion Exercise Manual)	32893-4
*Management System Booster Activities (1 pkg. of 47 Spirit Duplication Masters and Manual)	30727-9
*Management System Reading Achievement Cards (pkg. of 36 cards)	32895-0
Unit Decoding Pretests (Spirit Duplication Masters) for Levels 6-10	30724-4
Basic Card Set II for Levels 5-6	32575-7
Reading Progress Cards (pkg. of 100) for Levels 1-13	30873-9
Individual Skills Inventory Cards (pkg. of 100) for Levels 1-13	36397-7
Letters to Parents	37390-5

Level 7

THE DOG NEXT DOOR AND OTHER STORIES (hardbound)	30728-7
Teacher's Edition	30729-5
*Skilpak Booklet	30732-5
*Skilpak Spirit Duplication Masters (boxed set of 139)	33275-3
Studybook (Workbook)	30730-9
Teacher's Edition of Studybook	30731-7
Instructional Wall Charts	36738-7
Level 7 Mastery Test (pkg. of 36 test booklets, manual, key)	30739-2
Manual with Key for Level 7 Mastery Test (separate)	30740-6
*Management System Criterion Exercise Package (12 Criterion Exercise Booklets, 2 Criterion Exercise Record Sheets, 1 Criterion Exercise Manual)	32896-9
*Management System Booster Activities (1 pkg. of 48 Spirit Duplication Masters and Manual)	30744-9
*Management System Reading Achievement Cards (pkg. of 36 cards)	32898-5
Unit Decoding Pretests (Spirit Duplication Masters) for Levels 6-10	30724-4
Reading Progress Cards (pkg. of 100) for Levels 1-13	30873-9
Individual Skills Inventory Cards (pkg. of 100) for Levels 1-13	36397-7
Letters to Parents	37390-5

Level 8

HOW IT IS NOWADAYS (hardbound)	30745-7
Teacher's Edition	30746-5
*Skilpak Booklet	30750-3
*Skilpak Spirit Duplication Masters (boxed set of 142)	33276-1
Studybook (Workbook)	30747-3
Teacher's Edition of Studybook	30748-1
Instructional Wall Charts	36739-5
*Level 8 Mastery Test (pkg. of 36 test booklets, manual, key)	30757-0
Manual with Key for Level 8 Mastery Test (separate)	30758-9
*Management System Criterion Exercise Package (12 Criterion Exercise Booklets, 2 Criterion Exercise Record Sheets, 1 Criterion Exercise Manual)	32899-3
*Management System Booster Activities (1 pkg. of 44 Spirit Duplication Masters and Manual)	30762-7
*Management System Reading Achievement Cards (pkg. of 36 cards)	32901-9
Unit Decoding Pretests (Spirit Duplication Masters) for Levels 6-10	30724-4
Reading Progress Cards (pkg. of 100) for Levels 1-13	30873-9
Individual Skills Inventory Cards (pkg. of 100) for Levels 1-13	36397-7
Letters to Parents	37390-5

Level 9

INSIDE OUT (hardbound)	30763-5
Teacher's Edition	30764-3
*Skilpak Booklet	30768-6
*Skilpak Spirit Duplication Masters (boxed set of 108)	33278-8
Studybook (Workbook)	30765-1
Teacher's Edition of Studybook	30767-8
Instructional Wall Charts	36740-9
Level 9 Mastery Test (pkg. of 36 test booklets, manual, key)	30773-2
Manual with Key for Level 9 Mastery Test (separate)	30774-0
*Management System Criterion Exercise Package (12 Criterion Exercise Booklets, 2 Criterion Exercise Record Sheets, 1 Criterion Exercise Manual)	32902-7
*Management System Booster Activities (1 pkg. of 40 Spirit Duplication Masters and Manual)	30778-3
*Management System Reading Achievement Cards (pkg. of 36 cards)	32904-3
Unit Decoding Pretests (Spirit Duplication Masters) for Levels 6-10	30724-4
Reading Progress Cards (pkg. of 100) for Levels 1-13	30873-9
Individual Skills Inventory Cards (pkg. of 100) for Levels 1-13	36397-7
Letters to Parents	37390-5

Level 10

A LIZARD TO START WITH (hardbound)	30779-1
Level 10 Unit Books (paperbound)	32739-3

*Appears in Teacher's Edition of text

Code
Number

Reading 720 Continued

Pkg. of 1 of each of following:
Unit Book 1, Growing Is Quiet
Unit Book 2, Aha! A Sleuth!
Unit Book 3, Signs, Symbols,
and Codes
Unit Book 4, Long-Ago Yesterdays
Unit Book 5, A Touch of Magic—A
Touch of Wonder

Teacher's Edition	30786-4
*Skilpak Booklet	30789-9
*Skilpak Spirit Duplication Masters (boxed set of 142)	30790-2
Studybook (Workbook)	30787-2
Teacher's Edition of Studybook	30788-0
Instructional Wall Charts	36741-7
Level 10 Mastery Test (pkg. of 36 test booklets, manual, key)	30794-5
Manual with Key for Level 10 Mastery Test (separate)	30795-3
*Management System Criterion Exercise Package (12 Criterion Exercise Booklets, 2 Criterion Exercise Record Sheets, 1 Criterion Exercise Manual)	32905-1
*Management System Booster Activities (1 pkg. of 40 Spirit Duplication Masters and Manual)	30800-3
*Management System Reading Achievement Cards (pkg. of 36 cards)	32908-6
Unit Decoding Pretests (Spirit Duplication Masters) for Levels 6-10	30724-4
Reading Progress Cards (pkg. of 100) for Levels 1-13	30873-9
Individual Skills Inventory Cards (pkg. of 100) for Levels 1-13	36397-7
Letters to Parents	37390-5

Level 11

TELL ME HOW THE SUN ROSE (hardbound)	30801-1
Level 11 Unit Books (paperbound)	32740-7

Pkg. of 1 of each of following:
Unit Book 1, Setting the Pace
Unit Book 2, Where do stories
Come From?
Unit Book 3, Everywhere Tales
Unit Book 4, When the World
Was Young
Unit Book 5, Under One Sun

Teacher's Edition	30808-9
*Skilpak Booklet	30811-9
*Skilpak Spirit Duplication Masters (boxed set of 174)	30812-7
Studybook (Workbook)	30809-7
Teacher's Edition of Studybook	30810-0
Instructional Wall Charts	37520-7
Level 11 Mastery Test (pkg. of 36 test booklets, manual, key)	30817-8
Manual with Key for Level 11 Mastery Test (separate)	30818-6
*Management System Criterion Exercise Package (12 Criterion Exercise Booklets, 2 Criterion Exercise Record Sheets, 1 Criterion Exercise Manual)	32909-4

Code
Number

*Management System Booster Activities (1 pkg. of 35 Spirit Duplication Masters and Manual)	30822-4
*Management System Reading Achievement Cards (pkg. of 36 cards)	32911-6
Reading Progress Cards (pkg. of 100) for Levels 1-13	30873-9
Individual Skills Inventory Cards (pkg. of 100 for Levels 1-13)	36397-7
Letters to Parents	37390-5

Level 12

MEASURE ME, SKY (hardbound)	30823-2
Level 12 Unit Books (paperbound)	32741-5

Pkg. of 1 of each of following:
Unit Book 1, Which Turning?
Unit Book 2, On the Light Side
Unit Book 3, Days of the Gods and
Goddesses
Unit Book 4, The Web of Life
Unit Book 5, Wings for My Flight

Teacher's Edition	30829-1
*Skilpak Booklet	30832-1
*Skilpak Spirit Duplication Masters (boxed set of 158)	30834-8
Studybook (Workbook)	30830-5
Teacher's Edition of Studybook	30831-3
Instructional Wall Charts	37521-5
Level 12 Mastery Test (pkg. of 36 test booklets, manual, key)	30838-0
Manual with Key for Level 12 Mastery Test (separate)	30839-9
*Management System Criterion Exercise Package (12 Criterion Exercise Booklets, 2 Criterion Exercise Record Sheets, 1 Criterion Exercise Manual)	32912-4
*Management System Booster Activities (1 pkg. of 36 Spirit Duplication Masters and Manual)	30843-7
*Management System Reading Achievement Cards (pkg. of 36 cards)	32914-0
Reading Progress Cards (pkg. of 100) for Levels 1-13	30873-9
Individual Skills Inventory Cards (pkg. of 100) for Levels 1-13	36397-7
Letters to Parents	37390-5

Level 13

MOUNTAINS ARE FOR CLIMBING (hardbound)	30844-5
Level 13 Unit Books (paperbound)	32742-3

Pkg. of 1 of each of following:
Unit Book 1, Close-ups
Unit Book 2, Edge of the Possible
Unit Book 3, Beginnings
Unit Book 4, Songs Well Sung
Unit Book 5, To Reach Beyond You

Teacher's Edition	30852-6
*Skilpak Booklet	30855-0
*Skilpak Spirit Duplication Masters (boxed set of 190)	30856-9
Studybook (Workbook)	30853-4
Teacher's Edition of Studybook	30854-2
Instructional Wall Charts	37522-3

*Appears in Teacher's Edition of text

Code Number

Reading 720 Continued

Level 13 Mastery Test (pkg. of
36 test booklets, manual, key) 30860-7

Manual with Key for Level 13
Mastery Test (separate) 30861-5

*Management System Criterion
Exercise Package (12 Criterion
Exercise Booklets, 2 Criterion
Exercise Record Sheets, 1 Criterion
Exercise Manual) 32915-9

*Management System Booster
Activities (1 pkg. of 34 Spirit
Duplication Masters and Manual).... 30866-6

*Management System Reading
Achievement Cards (pkg. of
36 cards) 32917-5

Reading Progress Cards (pkg. of
100) for Levels 1-13.................... 30873-9

Individual Skills Inventory Cards
(pkg. of 100) for Levels 1-13 36397-7

Letters to Parents 37390-5

Reading 720/1978©

For students who need extra practice in basic reading skills.

Level 14A/1978©

TO MAKE A DIFFERENCE
(hardbound)............................. 35413-7

Teacher's Guide (includes students'
skills activities and unit tests) 35414-5

*Skilpak Booklet 36791-3

*Skilpak Spirit Duplication Masters
(boxed set of 84) 36730-1

Studybook (Workbook) 35415-3

Teacher's Edition of Studybook 35416-1

Level 15A/1978©

GIFTS OF PROMISE (hardbound) .. 35418-8

Teacher's Guide (includes students'
skills activities and unit tests) 35419-6

*Skilpak Booklet 36792-1

*Skilpak Spirit Duplication Masters
(boxed set of 84) 36732-8

Studybook (Workbook) 35421-8

Teacher's Edition of Studybook 35422-6

Reading 720 Supplementary Materials

Instructional Wall Charts

For use with 1976 edition

Level 3 36734-4
Level 4 36735-2
Level 5 36736-0
Level 6 36737-9
Level 7 36738-7
Level 8 36739-5
Level 9 36740-9
Level 10.................................... 36741-7
Level 11.................................... 37520-7
Level 12.................................... 37521-5
Level 13.................................... 37522-3

Code Number

Resource Activity Book/1976©

Paperbound 30868-2

Readalong Recordings/1976©

Level 3, A Duck Is a Duck (1 record) 33283-4

Level 4, Helicopters and Gingerbread
(1 record) 33285-0

Level 5, May I Come In? (2 records) . 33287-7

Level 6, One to Grow On (3 records) . 33290-7

Level 7, The Dog Next Door and
Other Stories (3 records)............... 33295-8

Level 8, How It Is Nowadays
(3 records) 33299-0

Level 9, Inside Out (3 records) 33303-2

Level 10, A Lizard to Start With
(3 records) 33307-5

Decoding Activity Charts

DECODING ACTIVITY CHARTS A
(Reading 360 and Reading 720,
Levels K-1) (8 charts, manipulative
pieces, Teacher's Guide)............... 25290-3

Teacher's Guide (separate)........... 25066-8

DECODING ACTIVITY CHARTS B
(Reading 360 and Reading 720,
Levels 2-6) (14 Charts, manipulative
pieces, Teacher's Guide)............... 25291-1

Teacher's Guide (separate)........... 25120-6

DECODING ACTIVITY CHARTS C
(Reading 360 and Reading 720,
Levels 7-8) (12 charts, manipulative
pieces, Teacher's Guide)............... 25293-8

Teacher's Guide (separate)........... 25127-3

DECODING ACTIVITY CHARTS D
(Reading 360 and Reading 720,
Levels 9-10) (10 charts, manipulative
pieces, Teacher's Guide)............... 25294-6

Teacher's Guide (separate)........... 25136-2

SAVE 20% by purchasing all four
sets including Teacher's Guide....... 36696-8

Supplementary Materials Bibliography Cards

Suggestions for books and anthol-
ogies for each unit and level, audio-
visual aids, professional materials,
directory of publishers................. 32962-0

My Phonics Practice Book

Write-in text for additional practice
and reinforcement in decoding skills 36381-0

Teacher's Edition of My Phonics
Practice Book............................ 36382-9

Ginn Word Enrichment Program/1979©

BOOK A
LOOK AND LISTEN.................... 35831-0

Teacher's Edition 35832-9

BOOK B
CONSONANT SOUNDS AND
SYMBOLS................................ 35833-7

Teacher's Edition 35834-5

*Appears in Teacher's Edition of text

Code Number

Code Number

Magic Circle Books Continued

BOOK C
VOWELS AND VARIANTS 35835-3
Teacher's Edition 35836-1
BOOK D
MORE VOWELS AND VARIANTS ... 35838-8
Teacher's Edition 35839-6
BOOK E
SOUNDS AND SYLLABLES 35841-8
Teacher's Edition 35842-6
BOOK F
MORE SOUNDS AND SYLLABLES 35843-4
Teacher's Edition 35844-2
BOOK G
WORKING WITH WORDS 35845-0
Teacher's Edition 35846-9

Magic Circle Books

Complete Magic Circle Collection

Save nearly $200. Buy the complete
collection—five copies each of 90
titles ($769.95 if all components
are purchased separately) 36693-3

Complete Library Units

Levels 1 and 2 Complete Library
Unit (5 copies of each title, Teacher's
Guide, 5 copies of the Skill Card for
each title, 2 copies of the Spirit
Duplication Master for each level) ... 30925-5
Levels 3 and 4 Complete Library
Unit (5 copies of each title, Teacher's
Guide, 5 copies of the Skill Card for
each title, 2 copies of the Spirit
Duplication Master for each level) ... 30926-3
Level 5 Complete Library Unit (5
copies of each title, Teacher's Guide,
5 copies of the Skill Card for each
title, 2 copies of the Spirit
Duplication Master) 30927-1
Level 6 Complete Library Unit (5
copies of each title, Teacher's
Guide, 5 copies of the Skill Card
for each title, 2 copies of the Spirit
Duplication Master) 30929-8
Level 7 Complete Library Unit (5
copies of each title, Teacher's
Guide, 5 copies of the Skill Card for
each title, 2 copies of the Spirit
Duplication Master) 30930-1
Level 8 Complete Library Unit (5
copies of each title, Teacher's
Guide, 5 copies of the Skill Card
for each title, 2 copies of the Spirit
Duplication Master) 30932-8
Level 9 Complete Library Unit (5
copies of each title, Teacher's
Guide, 5 copies of the Skill Card for
each title, 2 copies of the Spirit
Duplication Master) 30933-6
Level 10 Complete Library Unit (5
copies of each title, Teacher's
Guide, 5 copies of the Skill Card for
each title, 2 copies of the Spirit
Duplication Master) 30934-4

Magic Circle Components
Available separately

To accompany Levels 1 and 2

Levels 1 and 2—Package (1 each of
8 titles, Teacher's Guide) 24839-6
Teacher's Guide (separate) 24851-5
Skill Cards (5 copies of each title) ... 30560-8
Spirit Duplication Masters (2 copies
for each level) 30917-4
INDIVIDUAL TITLES (in pkgs. of 5)
We Need a Bigger Zoo! (Bunting) 24844-2
Walk, Robot, Walk (Mayer) 24841-8
Small Garden—Big Surprise (Adkins) 24843-4
The Bumbershoot (Hammond,
Winslow) 24842-6
Run! (Lane) 24847-7
Ride, Ride, Ride (Wiesbauer) 24849-3
Hide (Martin) 24848-5
The Park—The Park (Freschet) 24850-7

To accompany Levels 3 and 4

Levels 3 and 4—Package (1 each of
12 titles, Teacher's Guide) 24852-3
Teacher's Guide (separate) 24866-3
Skill Cards (5 copies for each title) .. 30561-6
Spirit Duplication Masters (2 copies
for each level) 30918-2
INDIVIDUAL TITLES (in pkgs. of 5)
Jill (Wiesbauer) 24853-1
Stop! Look! (Maynard) 24858-2
Cat (Martin) 24857-4
Duck in the Park/Duck in the Dark
(Begley) 24856-6
Where Is Zip? (Robison) 24859-0
Look with May Ling (Maxwell) 24855-8
How Can You Hide an Elephant?
(Martin) 24860-4
Do You See a Mouse? (Crume) 24861-2
The Pine Park Team (Seymour) 24862-0
"What Is It?" Said the Dog (Allen) ... 24865-5
In The Zoo (Lane) 24864-7
Inside the Red and White Tent
(Jensen) 24863-9

To accompany Level 5

Level 5—Package (1 each of 11 titles,
Teacher's Guide) 24867-1
Teacher's Guide (separate) 24880-9
Skill Cards (5 copies for each title) .. 30562-4
Spirit Duplication Master (2 copies
for the level) 30919-0
INDIVIDUAL TITLES (in pkgs. of 5,
except Blue Skies Magic)
Here Comes Pops (Wong) 24870-1
Tom Turtle (Hill) 24869-8
Say It Fast (Bunting) 24873-6
From My Window (Wong) 24872-8
The Big Green Bean (Wiesbauer) 24879-5
Box, Fox, Ox, and the Peacock
(Bunting) 24875-2
Said the Little Raccoon to the Moon
(Morton) 24876-0

Code Number

Magic Circle Books Continued

Imagine That! (Fife)	24874-4
The Little Elephant Who Liked to Play (Sellers)	24877-9
The Tail of the Mouse (Lexau)	24878-7
*Blue Skies Magic (Green)	29159-3
*(Not available in packages of 5.)	

To accompany Level 6

Level 6—Package (1 each of 12 titles, Teacher's Guide)	24933-3
Teacher's Guide (separate)	29816-4
Skill Cards (5 copies for each title)	30563-2
Spirit Duplication Masters (2 copies for the level)	30920-4
INDIVIDUAL TITLES (in pkgs. of 5) Boy in the Middle (Bond)	25393-4
Nine on a String (Bade)	25394-2
Paint Me a Picture, Mr. Pine (Kessler)	25395-0
The Nothing Zoo (Bohoy)	25396-9
The Pet Show (A. Johnson)	25397-7
Lines Make Me Lonely (Madian)	25398-5
Angel the Pig (Clapman)	25399-3
The Glerp (McPhail)	25400-0
Monsters that Move Earth (R. Johnson)	25401-9
Kim Ann and the Yellow Machine (Palmer)	25402-7
The Wind and the Sun (de Paola)	25403-5
Monkey's Tail/Rabbit's Cup (Turner)	25404-3

To accompany Level 7

Level 7—Package (1 each of 11 titles, Teacher's Guide)	24881-7
Teacher's Guide (separate)	29817-2
Skill Cards (5 copies for each title)	30564-0
Spirit Duplication Master (2 copies for the level)	30921-2
INDIVIDUAL TITLES (in pkgs. of 5) Yesterday I Lost a Sneaker (McPhail)	24882-5
William's Dog (Martin)	24883-3
Zoo Babies (Morton)	24884-1
The Opossum's Table (Hinckely)	24886-8
Dancing Nadine (Clapman)	24887-6
Tuloose the Miserable Moose (Hickox)	24888-4
Blast Off (Cain, Rosenbaum)	24889-2
Oliver Twister and His Big Little Sister (Yeo)	24891-4
Joey Tigertail (Comfort)	24892-2
Old Lion and His Friends (Brandt)	24893-0
Prince Littlefoot (Freschet)	24894-9

To accompany Level 8

Level 8—Package (1 each of 12 titles, Teacher's Guide)	24934-1
Teacher's Guide (separate)	29818-0
Skill Cards (5 copies for each title)	30565-9
Spirit Duplication Master (2 copies for the level)	30922-0
INDIVIDUAL TITLES (in pkgs. of 5) The King, the Dragon, and the Witch (Corsi)	25405-1

Code Number

The House on the Top of the Hill (Daem)	25407-8
The Magic Donkey (Joyce)	25408-6
A Horse for Matthew Allen (Smiley)	25409-4
The Long Line of Letters (Bartholomew)	25410-8
The Wonder of Change (Milgrom)	25411-6
So Many Henrys (Schatz)	25412-4
The Soapsuds Fairy (Palmer)	25413-2
The Moon—Jack and Jill and Other Legends (Branley)	25414-0
Through a Magic Glass (Russell)	25415-9
In a Time Long Past (Brandt)	25416-7
The Two Giants (Bunting)	25417-5

To accompany Level 9

Level 9—Package (1 each of 12 titles, Teacher's Guide)	24896-5
Teacher's Guide (separate)	29819-9
Skill Cards (5 copies for each title)	30566-7
Spirit Duplication Master (2 copies for the level)	30923-9
INDIVIDUAL TITLES (in pkgs. of 5) Mystery of the Blue Condor (Arden)	24897-3
Joey's Secret (McCracken)	24898-1
Robbie of the Kirkhaven Team (Rowland)	24900-7
A Gift for Lonny (Bunting)	24901-5
The Haganinny (Anderson)	24902-3
Jokes, Jests, and Jollies (Hoke)	24903-1
The Future Explorers' Club (Bendick)	24972-4
The Great Moon Hoax (Branley)	24905-8
The Runaway Camper (Conley)	24906-6
Susi Did It (R. Johnson)	24908-2
The Unicorn and the Moon (de Paola)	24909-0
The Valiant Little Potter (Berry)	24910-4

To accompany Level 10

Level 10—Package (1 each of 12 titles, Teacher's Guide)	22992-8
Teacher's Guide (separate)	29820-2
Skill Card (5 copies of each title)	30567-5
Spirit Duplication Master (2 copies for the level)	30924-7
INDIVIDUAL TITLES (in pkgs. of 5) Small Paul and the Bully of Morgan Court (Horvath)	25418-3
No One Need Ever Know (Read)	25419-1
Spring Is in the Air (Smith)	25420-5
School on a Raft (Beattie)	25421-3
The Dragon with a Thousand Wrinkles (Daem)	25422-1
Mags (Maclean)	25424-8
Beaver Boy (Dueland)	25425-6
The Circus Detectives (Abels)	25426-4
The Pine Tree that Went to Sea (Dueland)	25427-2
Dinosaur Dan (Reinstedt)	25428-0
The Troubles of Kings: Two Tales from Africa (Schatz)	25429-9
The Miller King (Tashjan)	25430-2

*Appears in Teacher's Edition of text

Reading 360 Continued
Tests/Charts (Levels 1-13)

Reading Progress Chart (pkg. of 100)
(Levels 1-10) 25502-3

Initial Screening Test (Levels 3-11
placement test) (pkg. of 35 test
booklets, manual) 25007-2

Specimen Set (manual, key) 25009-9

Tests—Specimen Set (manuals,
keys) (Levels 11-13) 21725-3

Reading Progress Charts (Levels
11-13) (pkg. of 100) 21724-5

Level 1 Studybook: Learning About Sounds and Letters

Studybook (consumable) 26473-1
Teacher's Edition 26475-8

Level 2

MY SOUND AND WORD BOOK
(1973©) (consumable) 25153-2

Teacher's Edition 25154-0

Practice Book (workbook) 21595-1

Teacher's Edition of workbook 21597-8

Test 2 (pkg. of 35 test booklets,
manual, key) 25241-5

Manual and Key, Test 2 (separate)... 25242-3

Level 3

A DUCK IS A DUCK (1973©)
(paperbound) 25155-9

Teacher's Edition* 25157-5

Skills Handbook (workbook)* 21605-2

Teacher's Edition of workbook 21607-9

Manual and Key, Test (separate) 25245-8

*Combined for Levels 3 and 4

Level 4

HELICOPTERS AND
GINGERBREAD (1973©)
(paperbound) 25156-7

Test 4 (pkg. of 35 test booklets,
manual, key) 25246-6

Manual and Key, Test 4 (separate)... 25247-4

Level 5

MAY I COME IN (1973©) (hardcover) 25158-3

Teacher's Edition 25159-1

Skills Handbook (workbook) 21614-1

Teacher's Edition of workbook 21616-8

Self-Help Activities (booklet) 21618-4

Teacher's Edition of Self-Help
Activities 21619-2

Test 5 (pkg. of 35 test booklets,
manual, key) 25248-2

Manual and Key, Test 5 (separate)... 25249-0

Level 6

SEVEN IS MAGIC (1973©)
(hardcover) 25160-5

Teacher's Edition 25161-3

Skills Handbook (workbook) 21623-0

Teacher's Edition of workbook 21624-9

Self-Help Activities (booklet) 21627-3

Teacher's Edition of Self-Help
Activities 21628-1

Test 6 (pkg. of 35 test booklets,
manual, key) 25250-4

Manual and Key, Test 6 (separate)... 25251-2

Level 7

THE DOG NEXT DOOR AND OTHER
STORIES (1973©) (hardcover) 25199-0

Teacher's Edition 25200-8

Skills Handbook (workbook) 21638-9

Teacher's Edition of workbook 21640-0

Self-Help Activities (booklet) 21644-3

Teacher's Edition of Self-Help
Activities 21645-1

Manual and Key, Test 7 (separate)... 25253-9

Level 8

HOW IT IS NOWADAYS (1973©)
(hardcover) 25201-6

Teacher's Edition 25202-4

Skills Handbook (workbook) 21650-8

Teacher's Edition of workbook 21652-4

Self-Help Activities (booklet) 21655-9

Teacher's Edition of Self-Help
Activities 21656-7

Test 8 (pkg. of 35 test booklets,
manual, key) 25254-7

Manual and Key, Test 8 (separate)... 25255-5

Level 9

WITH SKIES AND WINGS (1973©)
(hardcover) 25203-2

Teacher's Edition 25204-0

Skills Handbook (workbook) 25336-5

Teacher's Edition of workbook 25337-3

Self-Help Activities (booklet) 21667-2

Teacher's Edition of Self-Help
Activities 21668-0

Test 9 (pkg. of 35 test booklets,
manual, key) 25256-3

Manual with Key, Test 9 (separate) 25257-1

Level 10

ALL SORTS OF THINGS (1973©)
(hardcover) 25205-9

Teacher's Edition 25206-7

Skills Handbook (workbook) 25338-1

Teacher's Edition of workbook 25340-3

Self-Help Activities (booklet) 21681-8

Teacher's Edition of Self-Help
Activities 21682-6

Test 10 (pkg. of 35 test booklets,
manual, key) 25259-8

Manual and Key, Test 10 (separate) 25260-1

Level 11

THE SUN THAT WARMS (1973©)
(hardcover) 25207-5

Teacher's Guide 25208-3

Appears in Teacher's Edition of text

	Code Number			Code Number

Reading 360 Continued

Skills Handbook (workbook) (1970©)	21690-7
Teacher's Edition of workbook	21692-3
Self-Help Activities (booklet)	25816-2
Teacher's Edition of Self-Help Activities	25817-0
Test 11 (pkg. of 35 test booklets, manual, key)	21697-4
Manual and Key, Test 11 (separate)	21698-2

Level 12

ON THE EDGE (1973©) (hardcover)	25209-1
Teacher's Guide	25210-5
Skills Handbook (workbook) (1971©)	21700-8
Teacher's Edition of workbook	21703-2
Self-Help Activities (booklet)	25818-9
Teacher's Edition of Self-Help Activities	25819-7
Test 12 (pkg. of 35 test booklets, manual, key)	21709-1
Manual and Key, Test 12 (separate)	21710-5

Level 13

TO TURN A STONE (1973©) (hardcover)	25211-3
Teacher's Guide	25212-1
Skills Handbook (workbook) (1971©)	21712-1
Teacher's Edition of workbook	21716-4
Self-Help Activities (booklet)	25820-0
Teacher's Edition of Self-Help Activities	25821-9
Test 13 (pkg. of 35 test booklets, manual, key)	21722-9
Manual and Key, Test 13 (separate)	21723-7

*Appears in Teacher's Edition of text

Reading 360 Supplementary Materials

Decoding Activity Charts

DECODING ACTIVITY CHARTS A (Reading 360 and Reading 720, Levels K-1) (8 charts, manipulative pieces, Teacher's Guide)	25290-3
Teacher's Guide (separate)	25066-8
DECODING ACTIVITY CHARTS B (Reading 360 and Reading 720, Levels 2-6) (14 charts, manipulative pieces, Teacher's Guide)	25291-1
Teacher's Guide (separate)	25120-6
DECODING ACTIVITY CHARTS C (Reading 360 and Reading 720, Levels 7-8) (12 charts, manipulative pieces, Teacher's Guide)	25293-8
Teacher's Guide (separate)	25127-3
DECODING ACTIVITY CHARTS D (Reading 360 and Reading 720, Levels 9-10) (10 charts, manipulative pieces, Teacher's Guide)	25294-6
Teacher's Guide (separate)	25136-2

SAVE 20% *Get all four sets, including Teacher's Guides, for only $204.35* 36696-8

My Phonics Practice Book

Write-in text for additional practice and reinforcement in decoding skills	36381-0
Teacher's Edition of My Phonics Practice Book	36382-9

For further information, write:

Ginn and Company

P.O. Box 2649, Columbus, Ohio 43216
Or call, Toll Free: (800) 848-9500 (except in Alaska, Hawaii, and Ohio) and ask for customer service. In Alaska, Hawaii, and Ohio, call collect: (614) 253-8661.

Appendix C: Samples of Ginn Management Materials

Placement Test

Reading Progress Card

Pupil Profile Card

Individual Skills Inventory Card

Unit Test Record Sheet

Practice Exercise C

We watched a big balloon. It was flying across the ___(1)___ . Some people ___(2)___ in the balloon. They were high above the ___(3)___ .

1. ⓐ sky   2. ⓐ tried   3. ⓐ trees
   ⓑ letter   ⓑ rode   ⓑ guess
   ⓒ prize   ⓒ asked   ⓒ money

Practice Exercise D

Farmer Gage spent many ___(1)___ in his cotton fields. He was ___(2)___ the cotton. Farmer Gage hoped that he would have a lot of cotton to ___(3)___ . T___ ___ll of his hard ___(4)___ would be worth it.

1. ⓐ harms
   ⓑ flats
   ⓒ hours
   ⓓ benches

3. ⓐ kick
   ⓑ nail
   ⓒ rub
   ⓓ sell

Same format for practice and test

Independent reading selections

Placement Tests

Group tests are used when pupils first enter a program to help the teacher place each child at the appropriate level.

Level 8

Name _____

Gold is shiny and yellow. It is often used to make ___(1)___ . Getting gold is not easy. Often it is ___(2)___ deep in the earth. Workers must dig it out of the ___(3)___ .

1. ⓐ signs   2. ⓐ found   3. ⓐ jar
   ⓑ carts   ⓑ baked   ⓑ teeth
   ⓒ rings   ⓒ splashed   ⓒ ground

Some farmers raise bees. The bees live in hives and ___(4)___ honey. The farmers gather the honey from the hives. Then they take it to the ___(5)___ . Many people ___(6)___ honey. They like its taste.

4. ⓐ make   5. ⓐ ship   6. ⓐ yell
   ⓑ sell   ⓑ field   ⓑ buy
   ⓒ earn   ⓒ store   ⓒ roll

Tim wanted some cold juice. He put some ice in a glass. Just then the telephone rang. Tim left the ___(7)___ without his ___(8)___ . When he came back later, the ice was ___(9)___ . There was only water.

7. ⓐ thumb   8. ⓐ drink   9. ⓐ saved
   ⓑ kitchen   ⓑ corner   ⓑ tied
   ⓒ stamp   ⓒ bank   ⓒ gone

Level 8   Score (9) _____

137

Reading Progress Card

The Reading Progress Card provides a convenient and permanent record of the individual student's reading success.

- Space is provided for all Level Test and Mid-Level Test scores (Levels 1–15).

- File-folder format makes storage easy and provides a handy repository for records such as individual Score Summaries from level test booklets.

- Objectives are given for quick teacher reference.

File-folder
format

Name of Pupil _____

Year or Grade	Level of Instruction	Date Completed	Level Test Scores—Number Right Suggested Passing Score in ( )	List Specific Skills Needing Further Development and Recommendations for Future Instruction
1			Vocabulary (16) ___ Decoding (12) ___ Test Total (28) ___ Date:	Teacher ___ School ___ Date ___
2			Vocabulary (12) ___ Comprehension (5) ___ Decoding (14) ___ Test Total (31) ___ Date:	Teacher ___ School ___ Date ___
3			Vocabulary (12) ___ Comprehension (5) ___ Decoding (19) ___ Test Total (36) ___ Date:	Teacher ___ School ___ Date ___
4			Vocabulary (18) ___ Comprehension (6) ___ Decoding (25) ___ Test Total (49) ___ Date:	Teacher ___ School ___ Date ___
5			Vocabulary (24) ___ Comprehension (11) ___ Decoding (30) ___ Test Total (65) ___ Date:	Teacher ___ School ___ Date ___
6			Vocabulary (24) ___ Comprehension (10) ___ Decoding (33) ___ Test Total (67) ___ Date:	Teacher ___ School ___ Date ___
7			Vocabulary (29) ___ Comprehension (10) ___ Decoding (32) ___ Test Total (71) ___ Date:	Teacher ___ School ___ Date ___
8			Vocabulary (23) ___ Comprehension (18) ___ Decoding (31) ___ Test Total (72) ___ Date:	Teacher ___ School ___ Date ___
9			Vocabulary (36) ___ Comprehension (17) ___ Decoding (28) ___ Life and Study Skills (9) ___ Test Total (90) ___ Date:	Teacher ___ School ___ Date ___
10			Vocabulary (38) ___ Comprehension (22) ___ Decoding (27) ___ Life and Study Skills (11) ___ Test Total (98) ___ Date:	Teacher ___ School ___ Date ___

Mid-Level Test Scores

| 11 | | | Vocabulary (40) ___
 Comprehension (19) ___
 Decoding (20) ___
 Life and Study Skills (10) ___
 Test Total (89) ___
 Date: | Vocabulary (34) ___
 Comprehension (14) ___
 Decoding (12) ___
 Life and Study Skills (12) ___
 Test Total (72) ___
 Date: | Teacher ___
 School ___
 Date ___ |
| 12 | | | Vocabulary (40) ___
 Comprehension (19) ___
 Decoding (18) ___
 Life and Study Skills (15) ___
 Test Total (92) ___
 Date: | Vocabulary (33) ___
 Comprehension (14) ___
 Decoding (16) ___
 Life and Study Skills (11) ___
 Test Total (74) ___
 Date: | Teacher ___
 School ___
 Date ___ |

Vocabulary (42) ___ | Vocabulary (32) ___
 ...nsion (14) ___
 ...(13) ___
 ...tudy Skills (9) ___
 ...(68) ___ | Teacher ___
 School ___
 Date ___

...y (16) ___
 ...nsion (8) ___
 ...tudy Skills (8) ___
 ...(32) ___ | Teacher ___
 School ___
 Date ___

...y (16) ___
 ...nsion (8) ___
 ...tudy Skills (8) ___
 ...(32) ___ | Teacher ___
 School ___
 Date ___

Name of Parent _____   Pupil's Date of Birth _____   School _____

Date Entered School _____

Other Schools Attended   Dates

_____   _____

_____   _____

Reading Progress Card

Levels 1-15

Ginn Reading Program

Ginn and Company

The Reading Progress Card serves as a permanent record of each pupil's reading success. Read the heading atop each column and complete the requested information. Note additional significant information in the spaces provided on the back of the folder. Other records of pupil work such as the Score Summary pages from the Level Tests may be kept in this folder.

Level and
Mid-Level scores

Cumulative
record

Level 12

		Total Score	Suggested Passing Score	Pupil Score	
				Form A	Form B
Unit 1					
Vocabulary •	Word Identification	15	12		
Vocabulary •	Homophones	5	4		
Comprehension •	Main Idea	4	3		
Comprehension •	Supporting Details	5	4		
Decoding •	Prefixes *fore-, mid-*	6	5		
Life Skills •	Telephone Directory	4	3		
Unit 2					
Vocabulary •	Word Identification	15	12		
Vocabulary •	Classification	5	4		
Comprehension •	Comparison	6	5		
Comprehension •	Character	4	3		
Decoding •	Roots *spect, pend*	6	5		
Study Skills •	Directionary	5	4		
Unit 3					
Vocabulary •	Word Identification	15	12		
Vocabulary •	Synonyms/Antonyms	10	8		
Comprehension •	Sequence	6	5		
Comprehension •	Referents	5	4		
Decoding •	Suffixes *-en, -an (-ian), -hood*	6	5		
Study Skills •	Index	4	3		
Unit 4					
Vocabulary •	Word Identification	15	12		
Vocabulary •	Context Clues	6	5		
Comprehension •	Cause/Effect	6	5		
Comprehension •	Predicting Outcomes	4	3		
Decoding •	Prefixes *sub-, super, trans-;* Roots *scrib (scrip), port*	12	10		
Life Skills •	Directions	4	3		
Unit 5					
Vocabulary •	Word Identification	15	12		
Vocabulary •	Connotations	6	5		
Comprehension •	Author's Purpose	6	5		
Comprehension •	Fact/Opinion	5	4		
Decoding •	Suffixes *-ship, -ward*	6	5		
Life Skills •	Advertisements	4	3		
Unit 6					
Vocabulary •	Word Identification	15	12		
Vocabulary •	Multiple Meanings	5	4		
Comprehension •	Drawing Conclusions	6	5		
Comprehension •	Figurativ				
Decoding •	Prefixes com- (co-				
Study Skills •	Charts				

Teacher's Notes

Pupil Profile Card

The Pupil Profile Card serves as a permanent record of each pupil's reading success. Read the heading atop each column and complete the requested information for each unit of the Unit Tests.

Name of Pupil _____

Name of Parent _____

Pupil's Date of Birth _____ School _____

Date Entered School _____

Other Schools Attended _____ Dates _____

Pupil
Profile
Card

Levels 2-15

Ginn Reading Program

Ginn and Company

The Pupil Profile Card serves as a permanent record of each pupil's reading success. Read the heading atop each column and complete the requested information for each unit of the Unit Tests.

Individual Skills
Inventory Card

This is for effective record keeping; it tracks
all tested objectives by level.

Name of Pupil _____

Pupil's Date of Birth_____ School _____ Name of Parent _____

Date Entered School _____

Other Schools Attended   Dates

_____   _____

_____   _____

_____   _____

Individual
Skills
Inventory
Card

Levels 1-13

Ginn Reading Program

Ginn and Company

The Individual Skills Inventory Card serves as a cumulative record
of each pupil's skills development. Pupil progress is recorded by
use of the key listed below:

◸ INTRODUCED   ☒ REINFORCED   ■ MASTERED

▢ MAINTAINED — additional maintenance provided for long
term retention.

SAMPLE: Level 3

	Introd.	Reinforced	Mastered	Maintained
vowel digraph *ee*(ē)		☒	■	M
final consonants *m*(**m**), *d*(**d**)		☒	■	Ⓜ

*When skills are grouped, the teacher may indicate a specific element requiring
further development by circling the element.

If <u>maintenance</u> is provided for the entire skill group, place an <u>M</u> in the
"Maintained" box. ▢M

If <u>maintenance</u> is provided for individual elements, circle the <u>M</u>. Ⓜ

ABCDEFGHIJ087654321
Printed in the United States of America

Level 10 Grade/Year_____ Date Level Introduced _____ Date Completed _____

VOCABULARY	I	R	M	M
Word Identification				
Connotations				
Context Clues				
Classification				

DECODING	I	R	M	M
vowel digraphs — *ou*(*gh*)(ō), (ö), (ü), (uf), (ŏf); *au*(*gh*)(af)				
prefixes — *de, dis, en*				
suffixes — *ion, ish, ous*				
inflections — *f* to *ve* before ending *s*				
long words				

COMPREHENSION	I	R	M	M
Referents				
Drawing Conclusions				
Cause/Effect				
Figurative Language				
Character				
Fact/Opinion				

LIFE AND STUDY SKILLS	I	R	M	M
Alphabetical Order				
Dictionary				
Directions				
Forms				

Level 11 Grade/Year _____ Date Level Introduced _____ Date Completed _____

VOCABULARY	I	R	M	M
Word Identification				
Synonyms/Antonyms				
Homophones				
Multiple Meanings				
Context Clues I				
Context Clues II				
Classification				

DECODING	I	R	M	M
prefixes — *ex, non, im, in, mis*				
suffixes — *ist, ible, able, ic, age, ent, ence, ant, ance*				

COMPREHENSION	I	R	M	M
Character				
Sequence				
Main Idea				
Supporting Details				
Fact/Opinion				
Author's Purpose				
Figurative Language				
Cause/Effect				
Predicting Outcomes				
Drawing Conclusions				
Referents				
Comparison				

LIFE AND STUDY SKILLS	I	R	M	M
Alphabetical Order				
Dictionary				
Newspaper				
Maps				
Directions				
Telephone Directory				

Level 12 Grade/Year_____ Date Level Introduced _____ Date Completed _____

VOCABULARY	I	R	M	M
Word Identification				
Homophones				
Classification				
Synonyms/Antonyms				
Context Clues				
Connotations				
Multiple Meanings				

DECODING	I	R	M	M
prefixes — *fore, mid, sub, super, trans, ad, il, com* (*co, col, con*)				
suffixes — *en, an*(*ian*), *hood, ship, ward*				
roots — *spect, pend, scrib*(*scrip*), *port*				

COMPREHENSION	I	R	M	M
Main Idea				
Supporting Details				
Comparison				
Character				
Sequence				
Referents				
Cause/Effect				
Predicting Outcomes				
Author's Purpose				
Fact/Opinion				
Drawing Conclusions				
Figurative Language				

LIFE AND STUDY SKILLS	I	R	M	M
Telephone Directory				
Dictionary				
Index				
Directions				
Advertisements				
Charts				

Level 10 Unit 2

STRAND	Vocabulary						Comprehension			Decoding			Life and Study Skills			NOTES
OBJECTIVE	Word Identification			Classification			Cause/Effect			Prefixes de-, dis-, en-			Alphabetical Order			
SPS* / TOTAL*	12 / 15			4 / 5			4 / 5			6 / 8			4 / 5			
	Form A	Form B	Supplementary Pages	Form A	Form B	Supplementary Pages	Form A	Form B	Supplementary Pages	Form A	Form B	Supplementary Pages	Form A	Form B	Supplementary Pages	
1.																
2.																
3.																
4.																
5.																
6.																
7.																
8.																
9.																
10.																
11.																
12.																
13.																
14.																
15.																
16.																
17.																
18.																
Total Below Passing Score																
REINFORCEMENT* Booster Activities	7A, 7B			8A, 8B			9A, 9B			10A, 10B			11A, 11B			
Studybook (pages)	44, 47, 52, 56 59, 63, 68			53, 64			45, 57, 69			45, 58, 71			51, 55			
Resource Activity Book	see Index															
ENRICHMENT** Studybook (pages)	46, 50, 62, 66, 67, 72															
Resource Activity Book	see Index															

Alternate Forms A and B

Class scores at a glance

Reinforcement exercises

*Suggested Passing Score/Total Number of Items
**Additional Sources for Reinforcement and Enrichment Activities may be found in the Index to Core Strands.

Enrichment suggestions

Unit Test Record Sheet

This management tool tells at a glance just *how* each pupil is progressing. You can spot instantly when a child scores below criterion level, and whether this is an individual or a group deficiency.

ABCDEFGH 08765432
Printed in the United States of America